CELEBRATION
WOMEN

OUR GREATEST FEATS,
OUR FAVORITE STORIES,
OUR RICHEST LEGACY

EDITED BY

JOANN C. WEBSTER
& KAREN DAVIS

watercolor books™

SOUTHLAKE, TEXAS

UNLESS OTHERWISE INDICATED, ALL SCRIPTURE
QUOTATIONS ARE TAKEN FROM
THE KING JAMES VERSION OF THE BIBLE.

SOME PHOTOS COURTESY OF
ADAM BUCHANAN PHOTOGRAPHY
ADAMPHOTO@JUNO.COM

SOME PHOTOS COURTESY OF
CATHERINE KROEGER

INTERNATIONAL FABRICS COURTESY OF
SHERRY JACOBINI

A CELEBRATION OF WOMEN: OUR GREATEST FEATS,
OUR FAVORITE STORIES, OUR RICHEST LEGACY
ISBN 1-931682-01-1

COPYRIGHT © 2001 BY JOANN C. WEBSTER

PUBLISHED BY WATERCOLOR BOOKS™
P. O. BOX 93234
SOUTHLAKE, TX 76092
WWW.WATERCOLORBOOKS.COM

*To
our Mothers, Daughters, Sisters*

Special Acknowledgements

This book sprang to life thanks to the "Founding Partners" of the Global Celebration for Women, including the wonderful women from The Salvation Army, Campus Crusade for Christ, World Evangelical Fellowship Commission for Women's Concerns, Southern Baptist Woman's Missionary Union, Aglow International, World Relief, Women of Global Action (AD2000), Assemblies of God Women's Ministries, Pan African Christian Women's Association, Christian Women Communicating International, Hope for Europe, Lausanne Women, and the Institute on Religion and Democracy, inspired by the dynamo powerhouse, Winnie Bartel.

On a personal note, this book represents the combined efforts of loved ones and friends who have encouraged the life's passion and God's plan for all the lives represented here, as well as my own. What an honor to share the heartbeat of these mighty women of spirit, honor and courage.

I thank my mother, Dorothy Anderson York, for sharing with me God's gift of writing, as well as a zest for overwhelming projects. Mom, you personify the excellence of character the women in this book represent. Thanks also to Susan, Leigh Ann and friends at Harris Hospital who cared for Mom when she had surgery the Sunday before our Monday book deadline!

Joann Webster and Lynn Scarborough—thank you for answering God's "nudging" to ask me to participate. Thanks to Cullen and my son Chesley for making my work possible by doing more housework and cooking than anyone should have to do! And to my exhorter, Trey, who enthusiastically pushes me to "Do it, Mom. Just do it!" To his wife, Linda, and their children, Landon and Summer, who bring calm to the storm and are the joy of "Nana's" life. For Sasha and Anissa, whose teenage years are approaching, I am grateful you show some great characteristics featured in the following pages.

This book, and my life, would never have made it without my best friend since childhood, Sherry Jones Jacobini. Thank you, Sherry, for the all-nighters, for fighting the computer virus for which we could get no shot, and keeping this whirlwind organized. For Frank Jacobini, the builder par excellence, for sharing his "interior designer" with me so she could help mold the interior of this book, and in the process, work with God to fashion the beginning of the rest of my life.

A special thanks to LaTesha Hardy, Sheron Varin, Dr. Jayne Gardner and all the praying women from our Christian Women's Networking Club at La Cima Club in Las Colinas.

This book also would not have its focus and flavor without Kay Arthur's personal encouragement, and the help of Howard and Peggy Phillips, Morton and Helen Blackwell, Ed Fuelner, Ellen Grigsby, Janice Crouse and Beverly LaHaye, Lorry Lutz and her book, *Women As Risk Takers For God*, Madeline Manning Mims, and many wonderful Global Celebration friendships made and renewed.

Time and size prohibited inclusion of all 300 submissions we received, but Sherry and I sat in awe as we read each individual story. We learned from all of you.

My gratitude and thanks extend to my mentors, Sandy McKasson, Dorothy Kelley Patterson, Phyllis Schlafly, Katherine Dang, Ruth Smith, Betty Robison, Anne Murchison, and Olen and Syble Griffing.

We also extend thanks to publishers and authors who consented to excerpts, including Catherine Kroeger with her well-researched *No Place for Abuse*; to our editor, David Culp, for braving the final draft; and to Mick and Lynette for making beautiful words into beautiful art.

—KAREN DAVIS, EDITOR

Preface

We are women. Unique creations in the image of God, mothers of humanity, shapers of kingdoms, leaders of nations—we are women. Recognizing the imprint of the divine in our lives, we declare without apology, shame, reproach, or embarrassment: *We ... are ... women!*

The Apostle Peter said about Sarah, "... whose daughters ye are, as long as ye do well, and are not afraid with any amazement." What would a woman fear that would keep her from doing well? So much! Confronted by pressures—to speak, look, walk, teach, dress, parent, exercise gifts, display talents, become a certain kind of wife—women can become self-absorbed and self-conscious about everything, accomplishing nothing.

Faith is our shield, our antidote to fear. Faith that God makes no mistakes, and has divine purposes for us. Faith to see destinies fulfilled as we press into Him, our Father, King, Lord, Savior, and Divine Advocate.

Sarah is part of our rich feminine heritage. Acting on God's Word, Sarah transcended the natural into the supernatural. God told her she would bear a child in old age—the conception was supernatural, the birth was natural. Sarah's faith lifted her above the pain and discomfort of a season, to make her the mother of an entire people. Acting in faith, not fear, we become part of Sarah's lineage, her heirs.

Today, focusing spiritual eyes on the horizon, we see cloudy wisps of a women's movement forming. Not created as a backlash against injustice, nor based on man-hating, nor grounded in bitterness, this movement is forming by men and women who recognize women's achievements, feats and contributions over the centuries that leave us in awe and wonder. This is a movement that recognizes and celebrates who women are in Christ Jesus!

Over twenty years ago, my father, Ed Cole, became "the father of the men's movement," as he traversed the globe teaching men to accept responsibility, leadership, and stewardship. He taught men to treat wives as joint-heirs, to lead by serving, to father and raise children with purpose, and become accountable for actions both public and private.

How fitting, with the "new breed" of men today, that God would now raise up a "new breed" of women—women who are equipped, educated and encouraged to take part in fulfilling Christ's Great Commission and live up to our God-given heritage as His daughters.

My colleague, Karen Davis, and I present on the following pages Sarah's daughters. Women whose lives inspire faith, enhance dreams, and focus visions. Great women from Catherine of Siena to Rosa Parks, who have changed history, or stand in pivotal, world-changing roles on earth right now. Women who have honed their gifts and talents in speaking, writing, music, administration, government, sales, raising children, acts of hospitality and charity, and some by just being beautiful.

Thousands of years ago, a teen-woman on a donkey brought the Lord Jesus in her womb to Bethlehem. Just by showing up, shepherds and wise men flocked to her, to see the wonder of Jesus whom she birthed. Centuries later, Mother Teresa arrived in a war zone, determined to take children caught in the crossfire to safety. She carried the Spirit of the Lord Jesus within her, and caused generals from both sides to still their weapons to help fulfill her mission.

Whether it is Gloria Copeland with her speaking gift, Betty Robison doing charity, Madeline Manning Mims earning Olympic Gold, Dee Jepsen in politics, or Beth Moore writing books, the following vignettes, quotes and excerpts are from women who bring Jesus into the world around them.

Our purpose was not to include every woman of note, as we are each worthy of distinction and merit when we fulfill our destiny in Christ. Our purpose was to bring to your attention women you may not know—from the jungles of Africa, the fjords of the frozen north, and from the heat and stench of cities where women are bought and sold, and refusing sexual slavery is an act of heroism.

We included women of diverse backgrounds. Some were encouraged throughout life to do whatever God placed in their hearts. Others have overcome hardships so horrid as to be almost incomprehensible to the rest of us. They are women of diverse theologies, opinions, perspectives, social settings, cultures and historical eras, yet they are Sarah's daughters who have acted in faith.

As editors, Karen and I encourage you to learn from them, laugh and cry with them, share their highs and lows, and above all, gain hope in fulfilling your divine appointment on this earth. We are women! Women of destiny, women of faith, hope-givers. Women who carry Jesus into the world around us.

— JOANN C. WEBSTER, EDITOR

TO THE WOMEN
OF FUTURE CENTURIES

To The Women of Future Centuries, this record is now inscribed.

History shows that no nation can enslave its women, but it insures its own barbarism. In proportion as society advances in culture, women are freed from an unholy tyranny, and in that righteous freedom are able to do much for the world's advancement. Every civilized nation owes much to its women. And the student of history clearly perceives that the advancement of any nation is marked by the progress of its women; and therefore social, literary, and professional life in America may be clearly exhibited by a fair statement of the characteristics, labors, and successes of the women who have become in any way notable during the century which limits the history of the United States ....

Woman was, and ever is, in heathenism, abject and miserable. As a girl infant, she is scarcely permitted to live; her maidenhood has no incentives to purity and wisdom; and, when she becomes herself a mother, she may be seen often casting her own helpless babes to the Nile and its crocodiles, or becoming herself a sacrifice before the car of some juggernaut ...

One writer [Leo Miller, *Woman and the Divine Republic*] finds a signal illustration of this in the conduct displayed by woman on the occasion of the great tragedy of Calvary. He says, and truly if the record is complete and reliable, "Men alone clamored for Jesus' life; no woman's voice, thank God, was heard in the clamor. A man betrayed him, and for a very gross, material consideration. A man condemned him to death; the man's wife, in greater pity, begged to have his life spared. Men heartlessly deserted Him in the hour of His trial. Of His chosen friends and disciples, the men, in a cowardly manner, ran away and left him in the hands of his destroyers. Woman followed Him, shedding tears of sympathy and pity. Woman alone pressed her way through that murderous crowd to the very foot of the cross, and there poured out her prayers and tears in behalf of the world's dying martyr. Woman embalmed His precious body. Woman first greeted him when he had burst the bonds of death, and triumphed over the grave. Woman was first commissioned to go and proclaim the glad tidings of His resurrection. And woman today stands first and foremost in her Master's work,—the truest disciple and best representative of His divine life the world affords."

Mrs. Sarah J. Hale, in her admirable book, *Woman's Record*, says, "Woman is God's appointed agent of morality, the teacher and inspirer of those feelings and sentiments which are termed the virtues of humanity; and the progress of these virtues, and the permanent improvement of our race, depend on the manner in which her mission is treated by man."

⁊

PHEBE A. HANAFORD, 1882

SOURCE: *Daughters of America* (True and Company, August, Maine, 1882)

Women: Bringing Hope In the 21st Century

We stand at a moment of historical transition for women— a moment fraught with great opportunity but also enormous danger. As Executive Chair of the Commission on Women's Concerns for World Evangelical Fellowship, I have found as I travel throughout the world that there are distinctive trends that seem to perpetuate and worsen inequality, abuse, and oppression of women.

Women in every country of the world seem to deal with the same issues and concerns—immense poverty, abuse, lack of education for the poor, increased economic oppression, busy lives, domestic violence, and many other difficulties. As we move into the 21st century, I believe our greatest challenge as women will be facing the sufferings of women.

During the 1800s we read about the "golden era" of missions. One could safely say that women drove this golden era. Formal education for women was limited. However, they began to emerge as pioneers, becoming the force that instigated the modern missionary movement. Their focus was on service, and they emphasized family life, Bible studies, nursing, orphanages, and literacy. By the turn of the 20th century, more women served as missionaries than men. It was basically women in the homeland who supported them.

Something began to change for women in the early 1900s. Women were no longer viewed as equal partners with men in ministry and in service. "Proclamation evangelism" became the new missions paradigm, and women were not allowed to preach. This had an enormous effect on how women could function. In the early 1960s, this change resulted in the beginning of what has been called the feminist movement.

I remember it well—magazines telling me I needed value and self-esteem, which is something I didn't know I didn't have. Another paradigm developed, bringing New Age theology into the church. Women were told they could do it all, have it all, and be it all! The world's solution to our problems of stress was to:

ACQUIRE,

ACCUMULATE,

ALWAYS BE IN CONTROL OF EVERYTHING.

Today, the ultimate god is self-fulfillment, and what "I" want is the determining factor. On top of that, "righteous" living is viewed in terms of being tolerant. Demands, doubts, stress, and confusion seem to be overshadowing the lives of so many women. Their lives are fragmented, discouraged, and disillusioned by false expectations and unfulfilled dreams, leaving them feeling there isn't much hope anymore.

So, where do we go from here? I believe the answer to the greatest challenge for Christian women going into the 21st century is for us to become HOPE-GIVERS. To a world feeling there isn't much hope, we must dramatically change our thinking, our focus, and in any and every way possible share the HOPE of the Gospel of Jesus Christ.

I believe we are already beginning to see this unfold right before our eyes, during our lifetime. Women are the growth points of the church today. Statistics show that women compose 80 percent of the members of house-churches in China, 70 percent in Latin American Pentecostal churches, and 70 to 80 percent of African churches. Out of the 50,000 cell groups in the 700,000-member Yoido Full Gospel Church in Seoul, South Korea, 47,000 are led by women. Most of their 700 pastors are women. When I discussed this with Senior Pastor David Yonggi Cho, he remarked that he was not afraid of putting women to work, for by using women they were evangelizing all Korea. Clive Calver, international president of World Relief, states that some of his heroes of the faith around the world today are women. They are changing nations.

Proclamation evangelism has given way to "friendship evangelism," and who has more gifting in nurturing relationships than women? I truly believe women hold the key to the future of the Church. The future of missions today depends on relationship building. In a world that is totally fragmented, people are looking for acceptance, for love, for someone to care and to help. The only way we can make an impact against this hopelessness will be in making deliberate attempts at loving and caring for people—one person, one family at a time.

- TO A WORLD THAT IS OVERFLOWING WITH INDIVIDUALISM
- TO A WORLD THAT THINKS EVERYTHING IS OWED TO ME
- TO A WORLD THAT TEACHES US WE MUST ALWAYS BE IN CONTROL OF EVERYTHING
- TO A WORLD FILLED WITH PEOPLE SEEKING APPROVAL AND ADMIRATION
- TO A WORLD WHERE WHAT I WANT IS THE DETERMINING FACTOR FOR EVERYTHING
- TO A WORLD WHERE SELF-FULFILLMENT HAS BECOME THE ULTIMATE GOD
- TO A WORLD THAT EMPHASIZES PERSONAL CHOICE AND TOLERANCE
- TO A WORLD THAT HAS REJECTED ABSOLUTE STANDARDS OF RIGHT AND WRONG

- TO A WORLD THAT IS FILLED WITH DESPERATELY LONELY PEOPLE
- TO A WORLD FILLED WITH SUFFERING, POVERTY, WAR, PAIN, DEATH, SICKNESS, CRIME

It is time for women to rise up and meet these challenges, IMPACTING THIS GENERATION!

Whatever the sacrifice, we must get back to the basics, to what God has called us to be and to do as women and as the church. *"You have not chosen Me, but I chose you and ordained you to bear fruit ..."* (John 15:16). We are not sanctified for ourselves. Throughout history God has used women in mass spiritual revivals which have affected nations and generations. Women are an important key to bringing the hope needed in the 21st century and ultimately in building the kingdom of God.

This is why God's call on my life is to call into action the Global Celebration for Women. Women celebrating God and His work in and through us is vital as we enter this new millennium. My vision is to celebrate God and His work through women around the world in transforming nations and peoples with the power of Jesus Christ. This is:

- A wake-up call to the church, raising awareness of the immense suffering of women, giving all the tools and resources necessary for the church to rise up and respond;

- A time to continue the legacy of the strong, capable, godly women who have gone before us—and to begin mentoring the younger women, providing them with role models, examples, and ideals, empowering and challenging them to continue on with the vision;

- A rallying point where women come together with one purpose, sharing ideals and plans, to merge forces to wield influence, to affect change in their nations and their communities all over the world.

We are living in a moment in time that is so important we dare not squander it. History again will show how God sent His anointing. And—through the lives of women—He will affect nations, kingdoms, and the world! SO MAY IT BE!

WINNIE BARTEL

Winnie Bartel is the founding chairperson of the World Evangelical Fellowship Commission on Women's Concerns.

WOMEN OF FAITH AND PRINCIPLE

"Throughout history, women have played vital and pivotal roles in shaping society by promoting virtue and biblical values. As we stand on the shoulders of those women, we must keep our focus on God. He is working to transform the lives of women around the world—all of us flawed and ordinary women who are willing to be used for His purposes. He delights in lifting up unlikely people to build His kingdom here on earth."

JANICE CROUSE, PH.D.

A former presidential speechwriter, Dr. Janice Crouse co-authored A DIFFERENT KIND OF STRENGTH, *and is a senior fellow at the Beverly LaHaye Institute: a Center for Studies in Women's Issues.*

THE CHRISTIAN WOMEN'S DECLARATION

First and foremost, we are women of faith and principle whose Christianity is founded, not on human invention, but on divinely-revealed truth. This truth enables us to experience the redemptive, transforming power of Jesus Christ who made freedom and dignity possible for all human beings—for women as well as for men. Because we are created in God's image and the grace of God is extended equally to women, we can join the company of those women who first wept in the shadow of the cross and later rejoiced at the empty tomb. Because the Bible is the most effective force in history for lifting women to higher levels of respect, dignity and freedom, we join a historic succession of women whose Christian faith is forged from biblical truth and whose lives are shaped into Christ's image on the anvil of obedience.

SOURCE: Excerpts from www.beverlylahayeinstitute.org

STAND AND FIGHT BACK

Feminism no longer stands on uncontested ground. The vast numbers of women who have found empowerment through faith are ready to speak against the minority who have heretofore been the self-appointed mouthpiece of all women. The time has come to stand as Christian women and proclaim the Truth—Jesus Christ is the Liberator of women, not our oppressor. We intend to fight back on behalf of the next generation of women. We need not re-imagine our faith. We need only boldly declare it. In days to come, the feminists will find competition at the forefront of the debate over what women really want.

❧

WINNIE BARTEL,
responding to the CHRISTIAN WOMEN'S DECLARATION

A SENSE OF MISSION
BRINGS EMPOWERMENT

"When we women knocked on the doors of America's law schools, we were simply following our dreams, which seemed as natural to us as staying home and getting married was to many others. What empowerment is all about [is] finding something which infuses you with a sense of mission, with a passion for your life's work. I don't believe there is one path for women or one nature to fulfill. Real fulfillment, real empowerment is often different than we imagine and better than we plan."

ELIZABETH DOLE

Former head of two cabinet departments (Labor and Transportation), former head of the American Red Cross, former presidential candidate, wife of former Senate Majority Leader Bob Dole, Elizabeth Dole was one of 24 women in a class of 550 when she entered Harvard Law School in 1962.

SOURCES: *Ladies' Home Journal* speech, May 5, 1999; www.cnn.com/allpolitics

DARE TO LEARN

"Learning is not attained by chance, it must be sought for with ardor and attended to with diligence."

—ABIGAIL ADAMS, LETTER TO HER SON, JOHN QUINCY ADAMS; MAY 8, 1780

SOURCE: *Familiar Quotations* by John Bartlett.

TAKING CONTROL
OR YIELDING CONTROL?

"Today, we hear so much about women taking control of their lives, about learning to control others, and about finding personal fulfillment through our own efforts. But God calls us to different priorities. He asks men and women alike to find strength and meaning through serving Him and reaching out to meet the needs of others. God has promised that He will live and serve through us and that He will empower us in remarkable and effective ways."

BEVERLY LAHAYE

Beverly LaHaye is the founder and chairman of Concerned Women for America, which was founded to protect and promote biblical values for women and families—first through prayer, then through education and, finally, by influencing our elected leaders and society.

SHIRLEY DOBSON

The wife of psychologist and author Dr. James C. Dobson, founder of *Focus on the Family*, Shirley Dobson is one of America's prominent Christian women that others look to as an example. Mrs. Dobson's outreach to Christian women has included leadership roles in Bible Study Fellowship and other groups devoted to the study of Scripture. She has also served as director of women's ministries for a large evangelical church and continues to speak across the country about issues affecting women and families. She was a featured speaker at the "Renewing the Heart" women's conferences throughout the nation. In addition, Mrs. Dobson is a member of the board of directors for Focus on the Family.

Perhaps her most far-reaching ministry is the National Day of Prayer Task Force, which she chairs. Through the efforts of her team, more than 30,000 prayer gatherings are conducted by 40,000 volunteers across the country. It is projected that over two million people participate every year in this call to prayer for the nation and its families.

She is co-author, with Gloria Gaither, of two books: *Let's Make a Memory*, a book devoted to establishing family traditions that impact children for a lifetime, and *Let's Hide the Word*, which gives parents practical and fun ways to build Scripture vocabularies in their children. More recently, she and her husband co-authored a daily devotional book, *Night Light*.

CHANGING NEIGHBORHOODS AND NATIONS

CLARE BOOTHE LUCE

"There are no hopeless situations;
there are only men who have
grown hopeless about them."

Clare Booth Luce (1903-1987) was a leader in the free world's opposition to communism and an outspoken advocate of free enterprise. Devoted to her family, she came under the same kind of attack from liberals and feminists of her day that women encounter today when they are successful without espousing feminist ideas.

Mrs. Luce was the editor of *Vanity Fair*, an award-winning playwright, a prolific author, a foreign and domestic journalist, a congresswoman from Connecticut, the American ambassador to Italy, a widely admired conservative leader, as well as a loving wife and mother. Her personal and public accomplishments made it natural that the title *"The Woman of the Century"* was bestowed upon her after her death.

SOURCE: Clare Boothe Luce Policy Institute

WOMAN, WHY ARE YOU CRYING?

Mary straightened up as she turned to face Him, and the question Jesus challenged her with is one that resounds in our day: "Woman ... why are you crying? Who is it you are looking for?" (John 20:15)

Today, with all of our liberation and feminization and equalization and assertion and recognition, women are still unhappy! We are still "crying." The high rate of divorce and drug dependency, of abortion and alcoholism, of immorality and therapy reflect the tears of a generation of women who are looking for Someone. And our Lord's gentle voice still prods, "Woman, why are you crying? What's missing in your life? Why are you so empty? What are you looking for? Who are you looking for?"

Then the One Who was her Shepherd called her by name, "Mary" (John 20:16). Her head must have snapped up as her eyes focused sharply on the "gardener." We can only imagine the electrified shock that caused every taut, frayed nerve in her body to tingle as she recognized her Shepherd's voice and saw, with her own eyes, her Shepherd's face! As she clung to Him and felt His flesh and bones and life, she knew He was more than she ever had thought Him to be! Never again would she be empty or lonely, loveless or lifeless, hopeless or helpless, captured or condemned because He was alive!

ℰ

ANNE GRAHAM LOTZ

The daughter of Billy and Ruth Bell Graham, Anne Graham Lotz has been a powerful evangelist in her own right for more than 25 years.

SOURCE: AnGeL Ministries newsletter, summer-fall 2000; www.angelministries.org

HAVE WE BEEN FAITHFUL?

"When we stand before God,
He will not ask us if we have been successful,
but if we have been faithful."

—ELIZABETH WEIDMAN WOOD,
MISSIONARY TO CHINA

MY DISAPPOINTMENT
WAS HIS APPOINTMENT

I slid from the bed to the floor. Only being on my knees could resolve the anguish of my heart. I knew I had failed God. Obviously, my thinking wasn't clear. It wasn't my fault that the pericardium surrounding my heart was infected or that the amoebas I picked up in Mexico had weakened my body to the point that the doctors told Jack I should leave the mission field. Nor could Jack be persuaded that we ought to stay, "We're going home." That is it. There was no arguing with my husband.

"O Father, I feel like such a failure. I've brought a much-needed man off the mission field. You know all I want to be is a missionary …."

Little did I realize that my disappointment was God's appointment. The "d" of disappointment would be dropped and an *"H"* added. Over time, the space between the *His* and *appointment* would become evident—for in His sovereignty our mission field would move from Mexico to the United States, into 118 countries and 65 languages with more waiting to be included. God had something much bigger, much greater than we could ever conceive: Precept Ministries International (PMI).

My moment of conversion had come some years before my "moment of appointment" in Mexico. At the age of 29, after a marriage and a divorce, I searched for unconditional love, living an immoral lifestyle. All that changed July 16, 1963, when I fell on my knees and cried out to God, telling Him He could do with me as He pleased. His pleasure was to make me a new creation in Christ Jesus as He called me *beloved* when there was nothing lovely about me.

From the moment of my salvation, there was a hunger and thirst for His Word and His righteousness. Besides devouring the Word, I read biographies of great historical men and women. Through the Bible and these living epistles I caught a vision of what God could do through a man or woman fully surrendered, whatever the cost, to the pleasure of God.

My first act of surrender was to tell God I would return and remarry my ex-husband, Tom Goetz. Although I didn't love this talented and brilliant man incapacitated by manic depression, I knew God could change Tom even as He had changed me.

On the heels of my surrender came the phone call telling me that Tom had committed suicide.

It was hours spent in the Word that held me in that hour of crisis. I had a glimpse of God's character and sovereignty. The knowledge and understanding of God's character grew as God called me with my two sons to the mission field, then brought Jack Arthur into my life and directed us to Mexico.

I began to teach the teens who met in our home the book of Romans. At the same time, God introduced me to the inductive method of Bible study through Dr. Irving Jensen's writings. Those three and a half years in Mexico were like the Apostle Paul's three years in Damascus—years of uninterrupted learning and growth.

Then in God's timing He brought us to Chattanooga, Tennessee, where He gave us a 32-acre piece of property five minutes from the airport. Little did we realize 31 years ago that people from across the world would fly into a conference center for training in the inductive method of Bible study. Many came in response to teaching that went out in person, through radio, television and in over 40 books and 30-plus inductive courses for children, teens and adults in 65 languages.

One of the greatest truths men, women and children have come to understand through PMI is the sovereignty of God and the absolute veracity of His Word. People from around the world share stories of victory after victory. When people know God's Word for themselves they can stand fast in the midst of trials, believe God to heal their past, discover their spiritual gifts, and be equipped to serve God and His church for the furtherance of His kingdom.

The deaf, the blind, the seeing, the hearing, the young, the old, the uneducated, the educated, the imprisoned, the free, the incapacitated, the strong, those bound in sin, those set free, the lost, the saved—all have learned to study His Word. The Truth has not only set them free, it has sanctified them, set them apart to serve the Lord, with confidence and boldness—and with a oneness despite denominational differences.

The goal of PMI is men, women, children and teens living as exemplary followers of Jesus Christ, studying the Word inductively, viewing the world biblically, and serving the church faithfully in the power of the Holy Spirit. And it is happening all over the world.

℞

KAY ARTHUR

Kay Arthur's Precept Ministries International began as one-home Bible study for 15 teens and another for five women. To date, the ministry has reached 118 countries.

CHANGING NEIGHBORHOODS AND NATIONS

WOMEN OF THE EARLY CHURCH

Eusebius, an early church historian praises the daughters of Philip, who were prophetesses (Acts 21:8, 9). Indeed, the New Testament makes note of many devout women of the early church, such as Suzannah, Jesus' follower and disciple (Luke 8:3); Priscilla, a teacher (Acts 18:26); Phoebe the deacon (Romans 16:1); and Mary Magdalene, who first announced the resurrection (John 20:18).

Adapted from Lorry Lutz, WOMEN AS RISK TAKERS FOR GOD *(Baker Books, Grand Rapids, Michigan, 1997)*

TRAINED BY WOMEN, NOW TRAINING WOMEN

The Lord called me to Christian service at a very early age. As the "preacher's kid," I participated in all the Woman's Missionary Union youth organization programs. While the strongest mentor of my life was my mother, God also sent godly examples in Alma Hunt and Mrs. Frances Tyler. They were all instrumental in helping with God's mission and vision for my life. During these early years under the tutelage of godly women, I learned that God could use my special gifts and abilities in His Kingdom's work.

For 34 years I have been on the staff of an organization that has existed for over 113 years. As the Senior Associate Executive Director of The National Woman's Missionary Union, Auxiliary to the Southern Baptist Convention, my office is responsible for designing missions activities and materials for women, girls and preschoolers in our denominational churches.

It is thrilling for me to watch women and girls throughout the world as they are radically changed and challenged by God's voice through this organization. It has changed and completed my life to be involved in the work of the Lord with this wonderful mission arm of the Southern Baptist Convention.

%

JUNE WHITLOW

June Whitlow is senior associate executive director of the National Woman's Missionary Union, Auxiliary to the Southern Baptist Convention.

A MENTOR'S TESTIMONY

Colossians 4:5 says, "Make the most of every opportunity." This is the story of how an American woman did just that, mentoring a young North Asian woman while on a vacation trip!

Dorothy had three weeks holiday due. She prayed that God would direct her to a country where people knew little of God's love and where Bibles could not be accessed. She obtained one New Testament in the language of her chosen country and departed. After booking into a hotel, daily she walked with her one New Testament praying that God would guide her to His chosen one. One day, she gave the Bible to a young woman who had shown her the way to a tourist site.

The next day the woman knocked on Dorothy's hotel door and asked her to help her understand her new Bible!

Even though they had no common language, the two women communicated by reading Bible passages in their own language. Before she returned to the States, Dorothy led the young woman in a prayer to become a follower of Jesus. The new convert started a small reading group for 20 people in her home as she explained the Scriptures to them!

In just two and a half weeks, God had used Dorothy as a mentor for a stranger in a foreign land.

I have seen a network of 2000 women commit to telling others about Jesus. My passions include a young Christian women's mentoring network in Australia, a mentoring group for teachers, a women's Bible study in Sydney, an evangelistic outreach to people in the city's apartment buildings and our preaching ministry.

ℒ

ROBYN CLAYDON

Robyn Claydon is a Fellow of the Australian College of Education and an author. Her most recent book is DOORS ARE FOR WALKING THROUGH. *She is chair of the Australian Lausanne Committee, with a focus on training emerging leaders.*

BORN TO BE A PRINCESS

Every woman was born to be a princess. Our Father, God in heaven, is the ruler over all the earth. As His children, adopted into His family through our faith in Jesus Christ, the King of Kings, we are royal heirs to all of God's promises. Our Creator designed His daughters to be the glory of men and the mothers of all living things. We were the final touch of creation and the solution to loneliness in mankind. Why have so many women fallen from that place of honor and esteem?

SERITA JAKES, *THE PRINCESS WITHIN*
(ALBURY PUBLISHING, TULSA, OKLAHOMA, 1999)

Serita Jakes is the wife of pastor and author T.D. Jakes. She is co-executive producer of the stage adaptation of her husband's best-selling WOMAN, THOU ART LOOSED.

CARRYING THE "HEAVY END"

One morning in 1949 my fiancé and I attended compulsory chapel at Wheaton College to listen to Stephen Olford—then a dynamic young evangelist. We sat far in the back where we wouldn't have to listen, and where we could hold hands and chat. But something about the message that morning grabbed our hearts. Olford's illustration became the vivid picture that changed our lives forever.

"If you saw ten men carrying a heavy log—nine on one end and one on the other—which end would you help?"

We've been helping the end with only one person ever since. Missions became the passion of our hearts—the driving force in our lives—the obvious plan God had for us.

In 1954 Allen and I left for South Africa to teach in an African high school. In our naiveté and inexperience we thought this was a lifetime assignment. But even before the school could open, Apartheid's growing restrictions closed its doors. The school happened to be on "white" land and couldn't be used for Africans. Discouraged and homesick, we traveled to Johannesburg for some R & R—and God revealed His true reason for bringing us to Africa. For the next 22 years we established and developed a youth ministry for Africans in the center of the black township of Soweto outside of Johannesburg. *Youth Alive* trained sharp young blacks in the Word of God and in leadership—an unheard-of opportunity for the frustrated young people caught in the prison of Apartheid. Thousands found Christ and an exciting, vibrant life in spite of the political chains that bound them.

When the pressures of frustration and anger broke out into violence in 1977, we left at the encouragement of our black friends. "You're a danger to us and to yourselves if you come out to Soweto," they told us. By then we had a strong corps of young leaders who were able to carry the responsibilities. Today *Youth Alive* continues not only in Soweto but also in other parts of South Africa under African leadership.

In the years that followed our return to America, we continued to work at the heavy end—first, under the aegis of Partners International, encouraging nationals around the world to lead their own ministries. Then I became involved with a new movement—the AD2000 & Beyond, which sought to plant a church in every unreached people group of the world by the year 2000. In 1990 the movement's international director, Luis Bush, asked me to form a women's track as part of the AD2000 movement. I literally laughed at him. I had never worked with women's groups and had no interest in doing so.

I was writing a book, *Partnering in Ministry*, with Luis at the time. As I interviewed Christian leaders around the country I asked them if they thought the AD2000 movement had any future, and if a women's ministry would be viable. The positive response and encouragement I received overwhelmed me. This, they said, was the day of the women. "Go for it."

For the next ten years I had the most exciting experiences of my life as I developed a network of women around the world. Our goal was to mobilize, empower and train women to focus on the unreached people of the world—those who had never had an opportunity to clearly understand God's love for them through Jesus Christ.

When the movement began there were over 1800 unreached people groups identified—ethnic linguistic groups of more than 10,000 people with no church planted. Though the movement did not reach its goal by the year 2000, all but a few hundred of these unreached peoples had been adopted in some way by churches, organizations and missions.

The AD2000 Women's Track held more than 40 training programs in those ten years—everywhere from Cambodia to Jordan. I had the privilege of teaching in many of these, urging women to put their strength to the "heavy end" and help build the kingdom of God. Even though the AD2000 Movement closed at the end of the year 2000, our women leaders felt strongly that we must not let the network die or the movement dissipate. The Women's Track merged with another ministry, Global Action, and together we have helped to spearhead the Global Celebration for Women. I continue to work with the Celebration—putting my strength and energy to the "heavy end," where so few women have had opportunity to do so in the past.

᯽

LORRY LUTZ

Wife, mother, missionary, author, ministry leader, and mentor, Lorry Lutz has helped to disciple countless followers of Jesus—both around the world and in her own home. All five of her children are in Christian ministry. Her eight books include WOMEN AS RISK TAKERS FOR GOD *and a novel,* THE SOWETO LEGACY.

CHRISTIANITY AND DEMOCRACY

Despite what some feminists might argue, we women are beneficiaries, not victims, of the Christian faith. Indeed, there is overwhelming historical evidence that biblical faith has been the most effective force in history for lifting women to higher levels of respect, dignity and freedom. As we enjoy new freedoms in Christ, it becomes our privilege and duty to seek to strengthen and renew our families, communities, churches, and societies. Sometimes what I most want to say to American women is: "Quit whining!" We enjoy unprecedented wealth, education, and freedom. Out of our abundance, can't we reach out to succor our suffering sisters and brothers around the world?

꯿

DIANE LEMASTERS KNIPPERS

Diane LeMasters Knippers is president of the Washington, DC-based Institute on Religion and Democracy, an interdenominational organization that works for the reform of the U.S. churches' social and political witness. She has headed the institute since 1993.

FROM POVERTY AND DEFEAT TO WONDERFUL VICTORY

For more than 30 years, Kenneth and I have been on a journey of faith. But though some people may look at where we are today and think our life must have always been this way, the truth is, we didn't start out with great success.

In fact, a few months after we got married, we ended up without jobs or money. Our furniture consisted of a rented rollaway bed, a coffee table Ken made in high school shop class, and some borrowed lawn chairs. Because we had no stove or refrigerator, I cooked in an electric coffeepot and put food in a cardboard box on the back porch. We were thousands of dollars in debt, and I was miserable.

Then one day I picked up a Bible Ken's mother had given him for his birthday. In it she had written, *"Ken, precious, seek ye first the kingdom of God and His righteousness, and all these things will be added unto you. Matthew 6:33."*

That sounded like good news to me, since "all these things" was exactly what we so desperately needed! When I turned to Matthew 6 and read that God even cared for birds, I realized that He must also care for me. I said something like, "Lord, I'm giving You my life. Take my life and do something with it." I didn't know it then, but I had just been born again.

Soon after that, Ken was also born again. We had quit running from God and had begun our journey of faith.

The first big step in our new journey took us to Tulsa, Oklahoma, and Oral Roberts University, where the Lord prepared us for what was to come. There, in a Tulsa riverbed, God told Ken that He had called us to the nations. At the time, we hardly had enough money to drive to Fort Worth!

What we did have was the quality decision we had made to do whatever we saw in the Word, including Romans 13:8: "Owe no man any thing, but to love." It looked like we would never have anything if we didn't borrow, but God is faithful. We started tithing and became partners with Oral Roberts for $10 a month. Within 11 months, we were completely out of debt and on our way.

During that time, we started having our own meetings. I was happy to help Ken in the background. But I never had much to say and couldn't imagine myself ministering as he did.

That all changed one morning in the summer of 1979. We were out in the country. I had been on the porch praying, and I went inside to wash my hair. The Lord spoke to me and said, *I want you to start teaching on healing in every meeting*.

It shocked me. Although we had lived healed for many years, I had never thought of teaching someone else how to do it. I didn't want a speaking ministry, and I wouldn't have picked *me* to do it. But it was the most powerful thing the Lord has ever spoken to me, so I was obedient.

We held our first Healing School that year. The Lord said, *I want you to share what you know about being healed, because I want My people well*. Later He instructed me to start laying hands on people. It has been a tremendous blessing all these years to see people get healed and delivered.

God is such a good God! The journey with Him has brought me from a life of poverty and defeat to wonderful victory in Him.

You can have that kind of life, too.

Nothing that has happened to me has happened because of who I am. It has happened because of God's Word. If I could give you a present, that is what I would give you—the Word of God. I'd rather give you the Word than a check for a million dollars. A million dollars can run out quickly, but the truth of God's Word never ends. And God's Word will deliver you from situations where a million dollars can't help you.

In fact, I can assure anyone, anywhere: If you will give God's Word your full attention—and not be afraid of His will for your life—you will be happier and more prosperous than anything you could ever dream.

&

GLORIA COPELAND

Gloria Copeland is an author, teacher, and ordained minister who speaks to women's groups, prayer conferences and ministers' conventions world-wide. And with her husband, Kenneth, she ministers daily through television, the printed page, teaching tapes, meetings, and conventions.

POWER FOR THE JOB
HE HAS GIVEN US

God's Word reveals over and over again how much He cares about the smallest details of our lives. The Bible promises that our real value and the true meaning of our lives come from belonging to Him. He is not dependent upon our frail efforts; instead He will empower us and give us everything that we need to do the job that He has called us to do. Our challenge is to cooperate with what He is doing as He builds strength and character in our lives.

&

CHARMAINE YOEST

A political commentator and columnist, Charmaine Crouse Yoest teaches politics and the family at the University of Virginia. She is the senior editor of EX FEMINA, *co-author of* MOTHER IN THE MIDDLE, *and a frequent panelist on* POLITICALLY INCORRECT.

ON THE WAY TO THE RACE, A VICTORY

It was 1968, the Olympic Games in Mexico City, and I had come a long way, baby! Stricken with spinal meningitis as a three-year-old, I had been given a fifty-fifty chance to live. "And if she does live," the doctor had said, "she will be mentally retarded and physically never able to do what the normal child does." But Mother had prayed and given me back to God, Who had His own plans for my life. And in one way, the doctor had been right: I had never done what the normal child does physically! Now, a sophomore at Tennessee State University and a member of the U.S. Olympic team, I was the top runner in the world for the 800 meters.

No one could have guessed how my victory in the 800 meters in Mexico would affect one young woman from Yugoslavia named Vera Nikolic. Vera was one of the toughest 800-meter runners in the world. We had met the year before, and now we were in the same semi-final heat. The first four finishers would advance into the finals, so there was no pressure to run hard, just safe. When the starter shot the gun for us to go, the run was somewhat easy for me. I led the whole way. As I came through the finish, I looked around to count the qualifiers and to my surprise Vera was not one of them. In fact, she was nowhere to be found. Later that night I found out that she had been so pressured by her delegation to win the gold that she had a mental breakdown on the track, walked out of the stadium, onto the bridge that overlooked the track, and tried to jump off and commit suicide. I was devastated.

Two days later, I saw her. I was on my way to my finals, the medal race. She was leaving the games, being escorted back home to Yugoslavia. I was drawn to go to her, even though I was about to run the most important race of my life. When I reached her, my knees were knocking and my hands were sweaty. What do I say to someone who doesn't want to live? No matter how much I tried to encourage her, nothing seemed to get through. Did she not understand my English? Could she hear me? She just stood there with a blank stare on her face.

I began to pray inside, and I heard the voice of God gently telling me to share my faith with her. I looked at her and said with all the love I could muster, "Vera, I don't know if you understand what I am saying, but God created you one of the best athletes in the world. You can't give up now. Go home and find Jesus, your Creator and you will find Life." Suddenly, out of those dark, hollow eyes flowed tears down her face. Somehow, we had connected. I held her in my arms and cried with her. We parted and I went on to my race, becoming the first American woman to bring back the gold in the women's 800-meter run.

The next year, at a meet in Germany, I found myself being approached by Vera Nikolic's coach. I asked how she was doing. He began to weep. "Last year," he said, "when we left Mexico to return home, Vera was placed in a psychiatric ward for therapy. She never spoke for a long time. Then one day she said, 'Coach, Madeline was on her way to her finals, and came back.' I was so overjoyed to hear her finally say something. She has been recovering ever since." I was crying then as I realized that my destiny is to Run for Jesus, love the people He loved, touch the people He touched, and to be the ambassador He calls me to be. I will always run for Jesus anywhere He sends me.

&

MADELINE MANNING MIMS

Madeline Manning Mims won ten national indoor and outdoor titles and set numerous American records from 1967 to 1980. She was on four U.S. Olympic teams, three times as a captain. In addition to her gold medal in Mexico, she won silver in 1972 as a member of the U.S. 4 x 400-meter relay team. She has written an autobiography, THE HOPE OF GLORY.

THE PAIN OF STRUGGLE

*"Many Christians
want the excitement of a reply
from God, but not the pain
of the struggle."*

—EDITH SCHAEFFER

SOURCE: L'abri (Wheaton, IL: Tyndale House Publishers, 1969)

IT'S THE DYING THAT GETS TO US

Few parents are given the privilege to witness their child's first and last breath. God gave us the awesome opportunity of being Bryon's parents for twenty-one years. At birth, the doctors predicted that "it would be a miracle if he made it through the night," due to a rare, incurable skin disease called *epidermylosis bullosa dystraphica recessive*.

It *was* a miracle that Bryon survived the constant infections, frequent blistering, daily bandaging of his open sores and ulcers, numerous hospitalizations, and 15 major surgeries. Everyone who met Bryon was impacted by his courageous zest for life and great sense of humor.

Knowing that every day was a gift from God, Bryon rarely wasted a moment to complain and often talked about heaven. Even at the age of seven during a hospitalization for a viral lymphatic infection, he was concerned about dying. He blurted out, "Mom, I hope I don't die before you!" When I asked why, he replied, "Because no one in heaven will know how to change my bandages!"

I assured my youngster that he wouldn't need *any* bandages in heaven. We spent a long time discussing the benefits and blessings of eternity in God's presence. Healed bodies. New skin. No more hospitals. No more injections. No more pain. It sounded awesome.

Then very seriously he asked, "Mom, does it hurt to die?"

I paused and weighed each word. "Well, buddy ... sometimes people just fall asleep in the arms of Jesus and they don't feel any pain. But other times people are sick for a long time and it does hurt when they die."

Bryon stared at me with intense concentration. I could almost hear the wheels turning inside his brain. With an air of subtle finality, he declared, "Going to heaven sounds great ... but it's the *dying part* that gets to me!"

Bryon was right—it's the dying part that gets to all of us! Dying to self and natural desires. Letting go of our will and accepting God's sovereignty in all of life's circumstances. Paul expressed it so beautifully in Galatians: "I have been crucified with Christ and I no longer live, but Christ lives in me" (Gal. 2:20 NIV).

Many have suffered painful losses in life and will relate to Jeremiah when he reminds us in Lamentations 3:23 that "His mercies are new every morning ... great is His faithfulness!" Thank God for His fresh portion of mercy that He provides to us daily.

It has been almost four years ago that we said good-by to Bryon for the last time. His prayers have finally been realized: new, perfect skin; functional fingers and toes; a body that can play basketball, football, or baseball; and freedom from the constant pain he lived in. He believed strongly, even to the end, that God had the power to heal him here. But if He had other plans for his life—as Bryon said it so well—"Either way I still win!"

❦

LILLIAN SPARKS

Lillian Sparks is the director of the Assemblies of God Women's Ministries.

LOVE AND SUFFERING

"If you love, you will suffer, and if you do not love, you do not know the meaning of a Christian life."

℘

AGATHA CHRISTIE, NOVELIST, 1890-1976

SOURCE: *Bartlett's Familiar Quotations*
(Little, Brown and Company, Boston, 1855, 1980)

HOW WOMEN CAN ATTAIN INTIMACY

We are fashioned for intimacy. We long for love and a sense of true caring. Yet, because of the Fall, we are broken people living in a world of broken people. We move toward others, based not so much on what they need but rather on what we need, endeavoring somehow to slake the hidden thirst deep within our souls.

Our need for relationship is legitimate; it is there by God's design. To have healthy, functional relationships, however, it is essential that we sort out what God, our "Source," intended to be to us. Since the time of the Fall, the "Source" of the woman has been to find her value and being in man (husband, boyfriend, how men view her) while the "Source" of the man tends to be his work (career, job, what he produces).

One of the foundations being exposed today is the "desire of the woman"—the belief that her husband, or any man, can be her source of life, that he can meet her need for unfailing love, worth, security, and purpose. "Your desire shall be toward your husband and he shall rule over you," (Genesis 3:16b, NKJV) is not a part of God's curse, but rather a warning to the woman. Because she has turned away from God due to sin and is now looking toward the man in her life, for her life, he will "rule" her emotionally. She is "up" if things are going well. If not, she becomes hurt, discouraged, and depressed. Ruled by her relationship, or desired relationship, with a man—her heart, her "center," having been turned from God to man—she is not able to be the help for him she was created to be (see Gen. 2:18). She is drinking from a broken cistern (see Jer. 2:13). She has the right expectation, but the wrong source.

Whatever we think will satisfy our longing will become our God. Satisfaction found in a wrong source, a false god, is always temporary, doomed to failure and disappointment. False gods are addictive because we must come again and again for refilling; what they can give us is never enough. We become slaves to what we think will fill the empty wells inside of us.

The needs women so desperately want met—those for identity, worth, purpose, security and a perfect unfailing love—are "being" needs. God wants us to find our "being" needs in Him; no human can fulfill them. When we find our life in Him, we will discover we can let go of our demands on others. We can then begin to move in genuine relationship with them because they are no longer the source of our identity and security. Until this occurs, real intimacy cannot begin to take place.

When a woman's heart is turned—when she sets her desire back on God—a new freedom comes. The grasping in her voice and her attitude goes. She is able to move into relationship with members of the opposite sex based on wholeness rather than inappropriate neediness, hurt, and woundedness. As a wife, she is able to speak into her husband's life with more effectiveness because her worth and identity no longer depend on his response. When the woman stops looking to her husband for the needs he cannot meet, she frees him to meet the ones he can: the need for intimacy and shared responsibility for the marriage and family.

This is a key factor in what God is doing today in the hearts of women around the world. He is turning the centers of women, teaching them to deny themselves, their own wisdom, their own strength, and to find their Source in Him. God is teaching them to live by the "tree of life," the life of God in them. He is freeing them from depending upon the broken cisterns of their own making, and fashioning women anew, restoring the man's help to him.

ℒ

JANE HANSEN

An ordained minister, Jane Hansen is president of Aglow International, an outreach ministry that impacts families in 145 nations. This essay is taken from FASHIONED FOR INTIMACY, RECONCILING MEN AND WOMEN TO GOD'S ORIGINAL DESIGN, *by Jane Hansen with Marie Powers (Regal Books, Ventura, California, 1997).*

IS A STRONGHOLD
SPOILING YOUR EFFECTIVENESS?

A stronghold is any argument or pretension that "sets itself up against the knowledge of God." A stronghold is anything that exalts itself in our minds, "pretending" to be bigger or more powerful than our God. It steals much of our focus and causes us to feel overpowered. Controlled. Mastered. Whether the stronghold is an addiction, unforgiveness toward a person who has hurt us, or despair over a loss, it is something that consumes so much of our emotional and mental energy that abundant life is strangled—our callings remain largely unfulfilled and our believing lives are virtually ineffective. Needless to say, these are the enemy's precise goals.

≈

BETH MOORE, *PRAYING GOD'S WORD*
(BROADMAN & HOLMAN, NASHVILLE, TENNESSEE, 2000)

STILL IN THE FIGHT

"I will always be out here doing the things I do and I'm not going to stop talking about Martin and promoting what I think is important in terms of teaching other people, particularly young people, his meaning so they can live in such a way to make a contribution to our advancement and progress."

℘

— CORETTA SCOTT KING,
QUOTED IN EBONY MAGAZINE, SEPTEMBER 1968

Now, as in 1968, the year her husband, Martin Luther King, Jr., was killed, Coretta Scott King continues to carry on Dr. King's legacy and philosophy of non-violence, fighting racism, poverty, and war.

SOURCE: www.triadntr.net/rdavis/mlkwife.htm

WE CAN SPEAK WITH AUTHORITY

As women, wives, and mothers, we have incredible role models of faith and action in the Bible. Consider Hannah and Mary, the mother of Christ, who were both led by faith and love into lives they would never have chosen. Both were asked to do what was not obvious, what was extremely difficult, and that thing was the pathway to their deepest joy.

As Christian women, I believe we are called to do something difficult—to be salt and light in the world, which rejects and sometimes persecutes us. We can speak with authority when we proclaim in the secular culture that children are a blessing, a source of hope and joy. When women face unplanned pregnancies, the unborn children are not the problem. The conditions of the mothers' lives are the problem. The mothers need our love and concrete help to see the way through.

Whether helping someone else get elected who represents her views or running herself, the pro-life Christian woman is in a position to be a heroine to the culture. Granted, it is hard, and that is why her faith must be strong to follow her strong, biblical foremothers. Women can make differences and address issues men cannot approach.

&

MARJORIE DANNENFELSER

Marjorie Dannenfelser is Chairman of the Board for the Susan B. Anthony List and is a former staffer at The Heritage Foundation.

STOP AND HEAR

*"The voice of God is always speaking to us,
and always trying to get our attention.
But His voice is a 'still, small voice,' and we
must at least slow down in order to listen."*

EUGENIA PRICE

SOURCE: *A WOMAN'S CHOICE - LIVING THROUGH YOUR PROBLEMS*
(Grand Rapids, MI: Zondervan, 1962)

LEADERSHIP PROFILE
CORAZON AQUINO

"RECONCILIATION SHOULD BE ACCOMPANIED BY JUSTICE; OTHERWISE IT WILL NOT LAST. WHILE WE ALL HOPE FOR PEACE, IT SHOULDN'T BE PEACE AT ANY COST BUT PEACE BASED ON PRINCIPLE, ON JUSTICE."

Believing in Miracles

Cory Aquino Leads a Fairy-Tale Revolution, Then Surprises the World with Her Strength. So read the headline in Time magazine's 1987 "Woman of the Year" issue. Before her remarkable rise to the presidency of the Philippines following the assassination of her husband, Ninoy Aquino, Corazon Aquino was a sincere, honest homemaker with an unshakable faith in God Almighty. She wore the same yellow dress most days of her campaign. "She showed how one individual could inspire in others a [...] so powerful that it vindicated itself and changed a co[...]'s history," TIME reported. Friends from her childhood ca[...]er shy. She did believe in miracles, though, and the "shy" [...] a revolution with the army of God behind her.

"The absoluteness of that belie[...] Indeed, her very real a firmness that can turn into stub[...]ill prompts friends and sense that she is an instrument [...] again, as a 'mission,'" th[...] relatives to refer to her caree[...]ecurity men by acting a[...] magazine said. "She exas[...]e shield. Her sense of re[...] she were protected by [...]

accounts too for Aquino's uncanny patience, her willingness, while awaiting what she regards as the appointed moment."

When, as president of her country, Cory Aquino spoke before a joint session of the U.S. Congress, it was reported that "she received the most thunderous reception given any foreign leader in more than a generation."

SOURCES: www.time.com, www.thinkquest.org

CHANGING NEIGHBORHOODS AND NATIONS

HARRIET TUBMAN

"I always told God: I'm going to hold steady on to You, and You got to see me through ... Just so long as He wants to use me, He'll take care of me, and when He don't want me any longer, I'm ready to go."

≳

HARRIET TUBMAN

God evidently wanted Harriet Tubman (1820-1913) on earth for a long time. A slave who had escaped to freedom, Harriet Tubman was one of the most successful "conductors" of the Underground Railroad during America's pre-Civil War era. Risking her life, she led more than 300 slaves northward to freedom. During the war, she served alongside Union forces in South Carolina as a nurse, laundress and spy. After the war, she helped set up schools for freed slaves.

SOURCE: Page Smith, *The Nation Comes of Age*, volume 4 (New York: McGraw Hill Book Company, 1981)

A VOICE OF HOPE
AROUND THE WORLD

The principle of Christian self-government is fundamental for the liberation and protection of women and children, and without self-government genuine freedom from tyranny of the State is elusive for all. The rule of law, administered by democratically-elected authorities, helps ensure the protection of basic human rights such as freedom of expression, freedom of assembly, and the freedom to practice one's religious convictions.

Through my decade and a half of working with Congressman Christopher Smith, I have focused on the protection of such human rights in my meetings with officials from scores of countries including Albania, Armenia, China, Egypt, France, Nepal, Nicaragua, Peru, Romania, Turkey and Uzbekistan. The protection of women is often a subject of my meetings with officials and private sector activists.

In my work, I have been honored to help fight against the trafficking of women and children, to defend religious freedom, to press for the release of prisoners of conscience, to speak out against violence against women, and to condemn the torture of imprisoned or detained individuals. The people whose lives are fractured by the excesses of the State or physical abuse long to hear the message of hope and deserve the voice of an advocate.

&

DOROTHY DOUGLAS TAFT

Deputy Chief of Staff for the U.S. Commission on Security and Cooperation in Europe (commonly known as the Helsinki Commission), Dorothy Douglas Taft has served in numerous capacities in the cause of freedom around the world. She and her husband, Jim, live in Alexandria, Virginia.

PRAY GLOBALLY...

... FOR SLAVERY TO END.

Two million children are forced into prostitution every year, half of them in Asia. Almost 200,000 Nepali girls, many under the age of 14, are sex slaves in India. Asian women are sold to North American brothels for US $16,000 each, where they are often held in debt bondage for US $40,000. Thousands of women worldwide are coerced or otherwise abducted into forced prostitution or sold through other forms of trafficking in women. Mass rape is a strategy of war intended to worsen the enemy's humiliation and pain.

In specific instances, traffickers in Miami have received Asian children trafficked through Europe by Japanese and Chinese criminal gangs. Girls as young as 13 were trafficked from Mexico via Texas, into Florida, and held under debt bondage in brothels catering to migrant workers. A Florida professor was charged with transporting a boy from Honduras for sexual purposes, while passing him off as his son. International traffickers have been arrested in California, New York, and Toronto. Five Latvian women were trafficked to Chicago and forced into slavery in strip joints.

The age of girls involved in prostitution is dropping, from 14 to 13 to 12 years of age. Child prostitution in the US escalated in the late 1980s after new laws made it more difficult for officials to detain runaway children.

- Pray for sex slaves to be set free.
- Pray for slave traffickers to be saved, convicted in their hearts of wrongdoing, and to stop.
- Pray for laws throughout the world that will stem the tide of slavery.
- Pray for people, ministries and money to arise that can stop the growing tide of slavery.

TO BE EQUAL

"We have to be careful
in this era of radical feminism,
not to emphasize an equality of the sexes
that leads women to imitate men
to prove their equality.
To be equal does not mean
you have to be the same."

GENERAL EVA BURROWS

CHANGING NEIGHBORHOODS AND NATIONS

CLARA BARTON

"An institution or reform movement that is not selfish, must originate in the recognition of some evil that is adding to the sum of human suffering or diminishing sum of happiness."

Clara Barton (1830-1912) organized and presided over the American Red Cross. She provided supplies and care to American Civil War troops and served in hospitals during the Franco-German War. Soldiers gave her the title of "Angel of the Battlefield." She exemplifies the woman committed to greatness without recognition or remuneration.

SOURCE: www.historyswomen.com

GUARDING KIDS FROM PREDATORS AND PORN

As mothers, we know that with one click of a mouse any child with a modem has easy access to pornography, and that pedophiles have easy access to children. As a devoted mother and grandmother, my life is centered on my family. Thirteen years ago, I was a homemaker when the Lord opened my heart to the need to educate and equip women about protecting their families and communities from predators and pornography. From a homemaker I became a CEO and now president of Web Wise Kids.

My word of encouragement to all women is to be open to what the Lord might have for you. When He speaks, do not be afraid to go beyond the comfort zone. Step out, mightily in a world that lacks a moral and spiritual compass. If we, who have the mind of Christ, are not willing to boldly step out, who will?

MONIQUE NELSON

Through its web site and workshops, Monique Nelson's organization, Web Wise Kids trains parents, teachers and other caregivers to help children make wise choices on the Internet.

LEADERSHIP PROFILE

DEMARIS MILLER

Enemy of Red Tape

Cutting out needless complication is Demaris Miller's forte. As a U.S. government research psychologist, she was an expert in redesigning and evaluating federal personnel systems, receiving two Hammer Awards for her work cutting red tape. Today she tackles other meaty national issues, speaking and writing about the proper role of government, lower taxes, school choice, personal retirement accounts, a strong national defense, and pro-life and pro-family issues.

A two-time congressional candidate from Virginia, she learned the "language of the Potomac" when her husband, Jim, was the director of the U.S. Office of Management and Budget under President Reagan. She is a grandmother, a former high school science teacher and basketball coach, a former pediatric nurse, as well as a former government red tape cutter. Now in private practice as a research psychologist, she serves as a volunteer tutor for children in the District of Columbia Public Schools and devotes time to mentoring other women.

IT WASN'T ALWAYS A ROSE GARDEN

Because my Daddy had always told me I could do anything, I called four New York Stock Exchange firms out of the Yellow Pages and told them I wanted to schedule an interview. But,

1) I couldn't train in New York (usually required),

2) I did not have a degree in finance, and

3) I did not have any work experience.

In addition, it was obvious that I wasn't the male gender that dominated the field at that time.

The results: I made three appointments! When I went to the first appointment, on a Friday, they tested and interviewed me for over five hours. I was hired and started in training the following Monday — with 25 men for six months. Finance-related businesses have since provided me a high degree of career success. After all, my Daddy told me so!

It wasn't always a rose garden. After a heartbreaking divorce, I searched for the Lord in all the wrong places. Finally, at the age of 39 I gave my life to Jesus, who reminded me that "… all things work together for good to those that love God …" (Romans 8:28 NKJV)

I believe the moral decline in our nation is the breakdown of the family, the coarseness of our culture and poverty of values. From the depths of my heart, I know we as Americans are blessed that He has given us the privilege to live in a free country founded by those who were looking for more than freedom of religion. They spent hours journalizing their desire to form a Christian

Constitutional Federal Republic. This knowledge is lacking in virtually every arena of American society.

&

SARA DIVITO HARDMAN

Sara DiVito Hardman is president of a consulting firm and an elder at Church on the Way in California. The former owner and CEO of Hardman Industries, she is the founder and former chairman of the Christian Coalition of California and served as city of Los Angeles community affairs manager under two mayors.

KNOW YOURSELF

*"When one is
a stranger to oneself
then one is
estranged from others too."*

—ANNE MORROW LINDBERGH

SOURCE: *Gift from the Sea* (New York: Vintage Books, a division of
Random House, 1955)

CHANGING NEIGHBORHOODS AND NATIONS

CATHERINE OF SIENA

Catherine of Siena (1340-1380) refused to marry so she could serve Christ. One of the leaders of a spiritual revival in the 14th-century church, she was instrumental in convincing Pope Gregory XI to end the papacy's exile in Avignon and return to Rome to deal with the problems of the church. During the Black Death, she risked her life caring for the sick and left deeply moving accounts of her experiences in her book, *The Dialogue*.

Adapted from Lorry Lutz, WOMEN AS RISK TAKERS FOR GOD *(Baker Books, Grand Rapids, Michigan, 1997)*

JOY IN BEING SINGLE

When in high school I was voted most likely to have a "tribe" of kids. I never planned on being single. Yet, I found God to be my sufficiency. I have great joy in the midst of being something I didn't ask for. This joy of God brings a deep satisfaction—"way in my soul."

You need to know who God created you to be and believe it! The word of God says, "I will praise thee; for I am fearfully and wonderfully made: marvelous are thy works; and that my soul knoweth right well." (Psalms 139:14) You are wonderfully made, whether you're "made single" or "made married." Believe that, and believe that His hand is on your life.

☙

PAM DAVIS

Pam Davis ministers around the nation as Group Director for Campus Crusade for Christ.

THE BEST OPPORTUNITY

*"Single women usually have the best opportunity
of all to get an education and learn a profession.
They can be ready to step in if need be and
provide an adequate living for their family.
This is not a new 'pro-woman' attitude.
It is as old as history. The Proverbs 31 woman
was equal to any task."*

—NANCY CORBETT COLE, *THE UNIQUE WOMAN*

LEADERSHIP PROFILE

SUSIE WOLF

One Who Cares

Raised in a Jewish home, at the age of 19 Susie received Christ when her mother was dying of cancer. Till then her sights had been set on a musical career. As a girl she had trained as a classical pianist and was majoring in piano performance in college. But with her Christian conversion came a change of course. Now with Somebody Cares America and Turning Point Ministries, Susie has worked on the streets, in the jails, and on missions trips around the world.

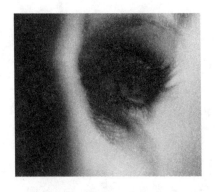

LEAVING A SPIRITUAL LEGACY

Whether you are married or single, childless or like the woman living in the shoe, you, too, have the opportunity to leave a spiritual legacy.

In Matthew 25, three servants were given different amounts of money, according to their abilities, to invest while their master was away. Upon his return they were called to account for themselves. The first and second servants, who had been entrusted with the most, had doubled their portions, and they were rewarded with more. But the third, who had only been given one talent (ancient measure of money) had dug a hole and left it there. His master was angry with him, and gave his portion to the two faithful servants.

Why are we given this picture? First to acknowledge that everyone is given a different amount to "invest" while here on earth. We cannot set this amount but only steward it. Second to show the importance of using fully what we are given. Just hanging on in life and trying to keep from losing ground isn't enough.

So what about you? Have you thought about your legacy? Every day, your beneficiaries surround you, and opportunities to bequeath time and energy are as numerous as minutes in a day. And as you invest into other lives, don't be surprised if you catch a certain smile or twinkle in the eyes here and there that reminds you of your own.

&

SANDY BLOOMFIELD

A former finance executive, Sandy Bloomfield is currently vice president of ministry and business development for SHINE Media, Inc.

SOURCE: Shine Magazine, May-June 2001

JESUS, OUR LIBERATOR

For too long, women have been held hostage, in their homes, churches, communities, cities and nations. Jesus Christ is the Great Liberator of women, and as women bow low as "Mary of Bethany," He raises us up as "Esther" to liberate other women. Now is the time for Christ the Liberator to set us free, to take our blood-bought place in His Kingdom.

TARA DORROH

Tara leads "At His Feet Ministries" in Spring, Texas

OPEN HEARTS, CHANGED HEARTS

God has given us music to open the heart, and His infallible Word to fill the heart and change it. Worship is a response to the Truth and our desire is to see people respond to God's Truth.

℘

ALICIA WILLIAMSON

Alicia Williamson is a singer, songwriter, and TV personality. Her work has been nominated for a Dove Award, the American Christian music industry's highest honor.

CHANGING NEIGHBORHOODS AND NATIONS

FANNY J. CROSBY

Blind from birth, Fanny J. Crosby (1820-1915) once thanked God for her blindness because she looked forward to the day when the first face she would ever see would be that of her Redeemer. Fanny Crosby wrote more than 6,000 songs, including "Pass Me Not" and "Blessed Assurance." She lived 95 years, finally seeing the face she had been waiting for on February 12, 1915.

LOVE SONG

"Jesus loves me–this I know
For the Bible tells me so"

&

— ANNA BARTLETT WARNER

SOURCE: AMERICAN HYMNS OLD AND NEW, *edited by Albert Christ-Janer, Charles W. Hughes and Carleton Sprague Smith, "Jesus Loves Me" (1858), (New York: Columbia University Press, 1980)*

LEADERSHIP PROFILE

GENERAL EVA BURROWS

"MANY OF OUR TROUBLES IN THE WORLD TODAY ARISE FROM AN OVER-EMPHASIS OF THE MASCULINE, AND A NEGLECT OF THE FEMININE. THIS MODERN WORLD IS AN AGGRESSIVE, HYPERACTIVE, COMPETITIVE MASCULINE WORLD, AND IT NEEDS THE WOMAN'S TOUCH AS NEVER BEFORE."

The People's General

Born in Australia to Salvation Army officer parents, Eva Burrows sensed a compelling call to ministry as a young woman. Since then she has visited more than 70 countries, and her speeches to the crowds there have been translated into 45 languages.

Commissioned a Salvation Army officer in 1951, she went to Rhodesia (now Zimbabwe), where she undertook an ambitious program for the training of black teachers. Her leadership acumen led to a series of appointments to head Salvation Army schools, eventually bringing her to the directorship of the Usher Institute, renowned in Zimbabwe as an outstanding girls' educational center.

Her subsequent performance in leadership posts in the U.K. and Ireland led to her being elected in 1986 as the General of The Salvation Army—only the second woman ever chosen as world leader of that organization. She retired in July 1993.

Perhaps the most significant of all of her accomplishments during her tenure as the movement's leader, was her effectiveness in leading The Salvation Army back into Eastern Europe, with work being re-established in former East Germany, Czechoslovakia, Hungary and Russia itself. She became known as "the people's general" for her willingness to spend time with individuals, whatever their status.

QUARRY ME DEEP, LORD

My prayer each day as I put my elbows on the windowsill of heaven and look into my Heavenly Father's face is, "Quarry me deep, Lord, that I may be a cleansed vessel through whom your Holy Spirit can flow unhindered." The Lord answers that prayer often, teaching me my most vital lessons through deep-heart struggles, disappointment and heartache. I have learned on the journey of obedience that He is totally trustworthy. He is able to do all He has promised and gives fresh faith for each day.

The Lord has given me a global focus — geographically, relationally, economically, politically, militarily, and spiritually. Through ministry among refugees destitute of all material blessings and faced with challenges beyond description, lepers separated from families and society, orphans, the blind and deaf-mute, my spiritual heart has been enlarged.

ℒ

BETTE CROUSE

Dr. Elizabeth (Bette) Crouse is assistant to the president of OMS International, an evangelical, non-denominational, faith mission.

CHANGING NEIGHBORHOODS AND NATIONS

MARIE BURGESS BROWN

Marie Burgess Brown founded and pastored Glad Tidings Assembly of God, across the street from Madison Square Garden. Spared from tuberculosis as a teenager, she dedicated her life to God, attended Moody Bible School and, though reluctant, moved to New York, the city where she would minister for 64 years, from 1907 to her death at the age of 90 in 1971.

THE PURPOSE OF LEADERSHIP

During this new millennium we will see women emerge in new roles of leadership and influence. They will recognize that the purpose of leadership is the *pursuit* of God. It involves interpreting life's circumstances from His perspective. It requires they ask the question, "Lord, for what purpose have you uniquely designed me?"

Their answer will not come from the systems of this world. Nor from well-meaning friends. Their answer will come as they sit at God's feet and allow Him to shape their character. It is the pathway to God's heart. It is the pathway to purpose!

ஜ

KATHY GISKE

Kathy Giske is executive vice-president of the Seattle-based Sentinel Group, a research and information agency that educates Christian and civic leaders on principles of community transformation. Her book, PATHWAY TO PURPOSE, *is being used to train women leaders in more than 20 countries.*

VICKIE HENRY

"Mystery Shopper" Shares Her Secrets

She showed early promise as a businesswoman, selling more Girl Scout cookies than anyone else in her Kansas troop at the age of 7. Years later she turned her instinct for customer service and her skill as a communicator into a ground-breaking business, FEEDBACK Plus, whose "secret shoppers" pose as customers of their clients' businesses and evaluate how employees do their jobs. Neiman-Marcus, Crate & Barrel, Planet Hollywood and hundreds of other companies have monitored their customer service with Vickie's professional feedback.

She's known as "America's mystery shopper," but Vickie Henry wants the source of her success to be anything but a mystery. A vocal follower of Christ and mentor of other Christian businesswomen, she is an active Board member of Fellowship of Professional Women in Dallas, helping other women achieve greater personal and professional success through godly principles.

PRAY GLOBALLY...

FOR WOMEN TO BE EMPOWERED ECONOMICALLY

Western women are making substantial progress at closing the employment, occupational, and earnings gaps.

The number of women-owned businesses with paid employees is growing dramatically. Approximately 50% of all women-owned businesses in 1992 were home-based while 56% of individual proprietorships were home-based. In a society that has been transformed because of women choosing to work outside the home as a matter of financial necessity, innovative ideas are giving rise to a best-of-both-worlds scenario.

On the opposite side, however, every poor female represents an equivalent of four hungry kids. In the developing world, women head one of every three families, except in Latin America and Africa, where women head one out of every two families.

"Is it not God's command to share your bread with the hungry; and bring the homeless poor into your house, when you see the naked, to cover them ..." (Is. 58:7)

- Pray for ministries that provide hungry children with food, clothing and shelter, and more importantly, for those who help the mothers of those children find and keep jobs.
- Pray for wisdom for mothers who struggle with work and financial demands as their hearts cry for their children at home.
- Pray for successful women's hearts to be moved to help other women move forward economically.
- Pray for men, and men's ministries who challenge men to act as stewards of their wives and the children they father.

ACT LOCALLY...

TO OPEN EDUCATIONAL OPPORTUNITIES FOR WOMEN

The gender gap in primary and secondary schooling is closing, but women still lag behind men in some countries of Africa and Asia. Two thirds of the world's 876 million illiterates are women. More than half of all U.S. college students are women, yet worldwide one of every three women cannot read or write.

More women than men lack the basic literacy and computer skills needed to enter "new media" professions. Women made up only 10.6% of all engineers at the turn of this century. In the new economy, women must be integrally involved in the information technological revolution, as well as mathematics and science-based occupations, whether from home or in a more formal setting.

- Encourage women with mathematical and scientific ability to chase their dreams.
- Pursue undergraduate and advanced degrees, to open opportunities for you as well as other women who will follow you.
- If you must work outside the home while your children are small, at least earn the most you can possibly earn by pursuing an education!

CHANGING NEIGHBORHOODS AND NATIONS

PAULA

Paula (or Paulina) (A.D. 347—404) paid the expenses of Jerome, translator of the Latin Vulgate, and provided women to copy manuscripts. By helping to produce a Bible in the language of the common people, Paula left a legacy that would last for more than 1,000 years.

Adapted from Lorry Lutz, WOMEN AS RISK TAKERS FOR GOD, *(Baker Books, Grand Rapids, Michigan, 1997)*

THROUGH CHRIST WHO STRENGTHENS ME

Can a single mother on welfare return to college, earn a degree and go launch a magazine? I did! After receiving Christ, I claimed the scripture, "I can do all things through Christ who strengthens me," and went back to college, attained my BS degree in marketing and launched an urban Christian magazine. The 1992 Los Angeles riots destroyed my business, yet the experience served as a springboard for my focus on cultural renewal. Not to be deterred by the trials, tribulations and riotous behavior of Los Angeles, I continued to persevere to empower other women in the welfare system to follow the biblical truth that had been proven in my own life. I was "pressing on for the prize" when I founded the Coalition on Urban Renewal and Education. CURE is a forum that promotes faith-based and free-market solutions on issues of race and poverty. Today, it is the leading free market think tank serving black America.

&

STAR PARKER

In addition to her work as founder and CEO of CURE, Star Parker conducts goal-setting workshops in housing projects, sponsors legislative briefings and empowerment conferences for inner-city pastors, and lectures at colleges and churches around the U.S.

LEADERSHIP PROFILE

BETSY BROWN

Traveling much of western and eastern Europe, plus North America, the Middle East and Southeast Asia, Betsy Brown has touched hundreds of thousands of people for Jesus. She leads Heartsong Ministries, which takes Jesus to the world, meeting people where they are, one by one.

AMID AFFLICTION, A DOOR OPENS

In 1987 I came down with a voice disorder that left me almost unable to speak for a number of years. This was a time of divestment of self, of losing my strongest gift—my clear, resonant voice—that I had used for His glory. It was hard to understand, hard to accept, hard to be diminished to nothing and still have hope in God. Yet—He was faithful, through it all.

It was during the midst of this physical struggle that the door opened for me to become president of the RENEW Network, a network for evangelical, theologically orthodox women within the United Methodist Church. RENEW also works closely with other renewal groups within the Mainline (or "Oldline") denominations. We are among those who are called to remain within these denominations and defend the faith and heritage the Lord imparted through them. Thousands within their pews have "kept the faith," despite the departure from it by many of their leaders. God sees them, He loves them, and He ministers to them through those who remain to serve them. Together we pray, "Restore us, O Lord, to a place where we will once again glorify Your name."

What a privilege is mine. His strength is made perfect in my weakness. He is faithful!

⅋

FAYE L. SHORT

In addition to her work as president of the RENEW Network, Faye L. Short serves on the boards of UMAction and the Ecumenical Coalition on Women and Society, both affiliated with the Institute on Religion and Democracy.

DONNA HURULA

Major Donna Hurula received a degree in Health Services and Gerontology from Spring Arbor College, Michigan, and became an ordained minister in The Salvation Army 35 years ago.

Her appointments include directing summer camping programs for children, family and older adults, leading women's prison programs, facilitating reconciliation between estranged persons and coordinating volunteer services.

Currently, Donna is Assistant to The Salvation Army President of Women's Organizations at the National Headquarters. She shares pastoral ministry with her husband, Bill.

LED TO LEAD

I feel privileged to be used by God at this hour to pastor a growing church. My husband and I want a church that offers such blessing that if anything were to happen, our society would miss us. We want to feed our members spiritually, and also train them, help them to be Christians who make an impact wherever they go. We want our church to be absolutely relevant and competent, especially in the area of music and the arts. We want to raise up Christians who are admired according to the Scriptures—"for this is your wisdom and understanding in the sight of the peoples who will hear ... and say, 'surely this ... is a wise and understanding people.'" (Deut 4:6)

&

YEOW-SUN HO

The Rev. Yeow-Sun Ho is deputy senior pastor of Singapore's City Harvest Church. Active in music ministry, teaching and preaching, she holds an advanced degree in pastoral counseling, specializing in emotional abuse and human relationships.

CHANGING NEIGHBORHOODS AND NATIONS

JULIA WARD HOWE

Her Words Rallied a Nation

"Mine eyes have seen the glory of the coming of the Lord," she wrote in the 1862 poem that, set to music, would be immortalized as "The Battle Hymn of the Republic." Julia Ward Howe (1819-1910) was the daughter of a Wall Street banker. Her husband, Dr. Samuel Gridley Howe, ran a school for the blind in Boston (later the Perkins School for the Blind), and together they published the anti-slavery journal *Commonwealth*.

When the ATLANTIC MONTHLY *published her poem in February 1862, Julia Ward Howe received $5. Her words' value to each generation of Americans since has been immeasurable.*

BECKY NORTON DUNLOP

Freedom Used Wisely

Currently vice president for external relations at The Heritage Foundation in Washington, D.C., Becky Norton Dunlop became well known in environmental circles as Virginia's secretary of natural resources. A leader in the free-market environmental movement and a frequent speaker on the need for a principled approach to environment policy, she is the author of *Clearing the Air*, about the challenges of achieving sound environmental policies in an atmosphere of liberty.

In the 1980s she was a senior official in the Ronald Reagan administration, serving as a special assistant to the president and director of his cabinet office in the White House, as well as holding high-ranking positions in the Justice and Interior Departments. She chaired the Interagency Committee for Women's Business Ownership and was appointed by Mr. Reagan as his personal representative to the Northern Marianas. In the private sector, she founded Century Communications, now headed by her husband, George Dunlop, a former Assistant Secretary of Agriculture.

THE SECRET OF RIGHTEOUS GOVERNMENT

"The government of the United States is acknowledged by the wise and good of other nations, to be the most free, impartial, and righteous government of the world; but all agree, that for such a government to be sustained for many years, the principles of truth and righteousness, taught in the Holy Scriptures, must be practiced. The rulers must govern in the fear of God, and the people obey the laws."

%

EMMA WILLARD, 1843

Historian and educator Emma Willard (1787-1870) was a leader in the movement to provide higher education among women. She founded schools in the U.S. and Greece, including a seminary for girls.

SOURCE: Rosalie J. Slater, *Teaching and Learning America's Christian History* (Foundation for American Christian Education, San Francisco, 1980)

STANDING FAST AGAINST THE RIDICULE

"We don't like to work with you. You won't compromise." My reply was, "You are so right. If any issue has a biblical statement or principle, then I will not compromise." Working on trying to get Abstinence Until Marriage curriculum into our North Carolina public schools, we were indeed dealing with steadfast principles. The Lord blessed and we were able to make funds available for every school system in North Carolina to teach Abstinence Until Marriage education. The latest statistics show that North Carolina has the lowest pregnancies for the unmarried adolescents that we have had in 18 years. My encouragement to anyone fighting battles on biblical principles, regardless of the arena, is this: Stand fast in the Lord, even when you are ridiculed and mocked. Never compromise God's teachings. Victory is seen in the name of Jesus.

&

ANN FRAZIER

Ann Frazier has spoken on moral and cultural issues and has led conferences in more than 20 states and several European and African countries on issues such as secular humanism, feminism, New Age movements and adolescent sexuality.

CHANGING NEIGHBORHOODS AND NATIONS
HANNAH MOORE

"Small habits well pursued betimes
May reach the dignity of crimes."

A gifted playwright and London socialite, Hannah Moore (1745-1833) at the age of 35 became a Christian activist. As a member of the Clapham Sect, she was one of Britain's leading voices for the abolition of slavery and the slave trade, for ending child labor, for improving prison conditions and for the establishment of Christian-based education.

Adapted from Lorry Lutz, WOMEN AS RISK TAKERS FOR GOD *(Baker Books, Grand Rapids, Michigan, 1997)*

SENTENCED TO DEATH FOR SHARING LIFE

A Christian couple responded to the advertisement in the newspaper and adopted the three-month-old baby that was "advertised." My unwed 16-year-old New Zealand mother said good-bye to me and I became the second child in a wonderful Christian home.

Throughout childhood my favourite game was school—*provided I could be the teacher*—so it was no surprise when teaching became my profession. Later, God challenged my life through two young New Zealanders who had been on a short-term mission trip. Two years of heart searching followed. In a short time, I was on to New York to work with Teen Challenge to begin discovering His dreams for my life. A summer of evangelism in Jamaica with Youth With A Mission followed. After training, I returned to New Zealand for two years before going to Europe. Thirty years later Europe is still my home and Youth With A Mission still my base organization.

From London to Kabul, Afghanistan, we rescued Western young people who were sick, dying and spiritually depraved— right in the streets of the capital! Then it was Albania when it was said to be the most closed land to the gospel in the world. With a friend we brought in some Christian literature to replace the "holy books" that were burnt in 1967. For this "crime" we were arrested, and sentenced to death. That was then commuted to life imprisonment; however, the police car we thought was taking us to prison, drove us to the border. We were handed our suitcases and told to walk home! Home was Switzerland, so it was some walk. Angels helped us on many occasions.

In October of this year, I will return to Albania to speak at an annual conference of our mission where national and foreign workers will attend from the eight bases established there. No doubt there will be other opportunities in this former Stalinist land which now embraces the good news of Jesus Christ.

The Mighty One has done great things for me. He has had regard for the humble state of His bondslave. Holy is His name.

%

REONA JOLY

Reona has recounted her adventures in a book, TOMORROW YOU DIE.

LEADERSHIP PROFILE

KATHERINE KEHLER

*"What I would want my grandchildren
to know one day is that I tried my best to reach
as many people as possible with the Gospel."*

A Grandmother Gives Birth to an Internet Ministry

It's not every day that a grandma pioneers an Internet endeavor. But Katherine Kehler, executive director of Women Today Online, an Internet ministry of Campus Crusade for Christ, Canada, is no ordinary grandmother. She launched womentoday-magazine.com in 1995, and it was soon voted as one of the top ten women's magazines on the Web. In 2000, more than 4 million women from 155 countries visited the web sites of Women Today Online. Between July 2000 and June 2001 nearly 300,000 women were discipled through the ministry, and almost 10,000 prayed to receive Christ.

Women Today Online wasn't Katherine's first startup. In 1976, she founded Canadian Prayer Alert, a ministry that mobilized prayer for government leaders across Canada. And in the early 90s, she launched *Women Today* the magazine forerunner of Women Today Online.

ABSTINENCE:
GOOD NEWS FOR GIRLS

I am here to say, from first-hand experience teaching the Best Friends curriculum over 10 years, that adolescent girls want to hear the abstinence message and will respond when it is offered in a developmentally sound and educational manner.

Through Best Friends, we provide a character-building curriculum. And, it works. An independent study of Best Friends girls attending D.C. public schools found a 1% pregnancy rate, compared to 26% among their peers. Four percent of Best Friends girls had experienced sexual intercourse by age 15, compared to 63% of their peers. Nationally, results are similar.

᠘

MARY ELAYNE GLOVER BENNETT

Mary Elayne Glover Bennett is founder and executive director of Best Friends Foundation, based in Washington, D.C. Her husband, Bill Bennett, is the author of the bestseller, BOOK OF VIRTUES.

THE BIBLE AND CIVIL LIBERTY

"The Bible is the only source of man's knowledge of how to obtain and maintain Christian civil liberty, and history shows that according to the degree the Bible has been received by the individual and its contents related to all aspects of his life, has Christian civil freedom risen or declined."

$\wp$

VERNA HALL, FROM HER INTRODUCTION
TO *THE CHRISTIAN HISTORY OF THE AMERICAN
REVOLUTION*, 1975

Considered to be one of the mothers of the resurgence in Christian education in recent generations, Verna Marie Hall (1912-1987) conducted pioneering work in researching and teaching the Christian principles underlying constitutional government and free markets. She co-founded the Foundation for American Christian Education.

ROSALIE SLATER

Carrying the Torch of Christian Education

She was Verna Hall's protégée, became her colleague, and today, in her 80s, remains one of America's leading voices for Christian education. With Verna Hall's writings on Christian self-government as her foundation, Rosalie Slater discerned the educational philosophy that undergirds Christian civil liberty and defined its providential view of history—the hand of God in the life of individuals and nations. Her seminal teaching guide for that philosophy, *Teaching and Learning America's Christian history: the Principle Approach* is now in its tenth printing.

Choosing in middle age to change careers and become a teacher, Rosalie Slater attended Stanford University, where she became concerned about the "progressive" system of education then being disseminated in the United States. Why, she wondered, did it appear to be contrary to what she, as a Christian, knew to be true about learning—that God is the Author of truth and the source of true learning? A 1959 trip to study the Soviet education system, highly regarded within the progressive movement, heightened her concern. Joining Verna Hall's constitutional study group in San Francisco, Rosalie learned that every form of government has its philosophy of education, and that progressive education was the educational philosophy of socialism. She had witnessed that Soviet education deliberately produced communism, and now she was startled to observe that progressive education was strangling the source of our liberty—the character of Christian self-government.

From this revelation grew Rosalie's life's work. She began to travel the nation with Verna Hall, doing research, holding seminars, encouraging schools and individuals, pastors and study groups. They established the Foundation for American Christian Education in 1964, an organization Rosalie still heads today. Founding pilot schools, developing curricula that are today used around the world, authoring books for teachers and parents, rediscovering gems of the past such as Noah Webster's 1828 dictionary —Rosalie Slater has helped changed the course of education in America and beyond.

Adapted from a biographical essay by Carole Adams, secretary-treasurer of the Foundation for American Christian Education and founder of StoneBridge School in Chesapeake, Virginia.

NEW LIFE IN EUROPE

In Germany at "Worship 2000," more than 10,000 young people, ages up to 21 years old, stood on their feet praising and worshipping the Lord ten to twelve hours at a time for a period of 72 hours. The call came for salvation and thousands came forward to give their life to Christ. This was a serious commitment to each young person who lay prone before the throne of Grace. One young man said it for all of them: "We know that when we answer a call to salvation in this nation [Germany] that it means we will be called to go to the [other] nations to spread the gospel." Still the young people were relentless and undaunted by the obvious lifetime commitment they were making for the sake of the gospel to be able to continually praise the Lord.

&

BETH ALVES

Beth Alves is an author, prayer leader and frequent speaker at international events.

CHANGING NEIGHBORHOODS AND NATIONS

SOJOURNER TRUTH

"When I left the house of bondage, I left everything behind. I wanted to keep nothing of Egypt on me, and so I went to the Lord and asked him to give me a new name ... I set up my banner, and then I sing, and then folks always comes up 'round me, and then ... I tells them about Jesus."

Sojourner Truth (1797-1883) wandered the North fervently preaching for emancipation of slaves and for women's suffrage. Often on her journeys, she would lie all night in the forest communing with God. Born in slavery in the state of New York and given the name Isabella, she was traded to several families as a child and married a fellow slave at age 14. She was freed in 1827. In 1843, Isabella had a spiritual revelation, "a voice from Heaven," and changed her name to Sojourner Truth to reflect the lifestyle and the message she believed God had given her.

SOURCES: Page Smith, *The Nation Comes of Age* (McGraw-Hill, New York, 1981), Vol. 4; Peter Marshall and David Manuel, *The Glory of America* (Garborg's Heart'N Home, Inc., Bloomington, Minnesota, 1991)

LEADERSHIP PROFILE

MARTHA WILLIAMSON

A Voice Crying in the "Vast Wasteland"

Maybe television isn't quite the "vast wasteland" it has been called. As executive producer of the CBS dramas *Touched By An Angel* and *Promised Land*, Martha Williamson is only the second woman to solely executive produce two hour-long dramas simultaneously on U.S. network television.

With *Touched By An Angel* Martha has had a notable impact on television and, in particular, the dramatic genre. According to the *Los Angeles Times*, which profiled her in an extensive Sunday magazine cover story, she is "the force behind the uncommon hour-long series ... giving her something in common with [powerful producers] Steven Bochco, David E. Kelley, Aaron Spelling and Chris Carter."

SOURCE: Pax TV

PRAY GLOBALLY...

FOR THE MEDIA THAT HELPS CREATE AND PROPEL PUBLIC OPINION

Years ago, sixty media firms controlled three-quarters of the newspapers, magazines, radio and TV stations in the U.S. Fifteen years later, the concentration of ownership was down to twenty firms that were gobbling up media outlets around the world. Today, mergers, acquisitions and cooperation between companies that normally compete with each other have created a near monopolistic control over the information and images disseminated in the mass media, which shape public opinion and morality.

- Pray for the accuracy of the messages the world receives in the news media.
- Pray to influence the intrinsic message of morality that film and music producers deliver daily to our children.
- Pray for advertisers to have yours and your child's mental health and morality in mind when they sell products.
- Pray to dispel and diffuse the old adage that "sex sells," which exploits women.
- Pray for corporations to see bottom-line profits when they use responsible messages in advertising and program content.
- Pray for a backlash against scenes depicting sexual promiscuity, and for a growing demand for humorous and intellectually stimulating dialogue.

SELF-IMAGE

"Jesus shows us that our self-image,
our sense of worth, our understanding
of who we are must be rooted in God's Word.
How we happen to feel about ourselves
on a particular morning
has nothing to do with it."

—ANNE ORTLUND

SOURCE: Disciplines of the Heart (Dallas, TX: Word Books, 1987)

ACT LOCALLY...

ON THE MEDIA MESSAGES IN YOUR AREA

Every five to seven years, United States television and radio stations come up for license renewal before the Federal Communications Commission. These licenses are a public trust; they are a privilege for radio and TV stations. Citizens are allowed to challenge the license renewal of TV and radio stations which demonstrate:

- station discrimination,
- lack of diversity in reports,
- failure to address local needs,
- a violation of the public trust.

Almost no challenges are ever launched.

As a result of the near monopoly ownership of U.S. media today, individuals who control the mass media are more identifiable than ever. As a concerned consumer, you can exert pressure for more responsible messages in a focused, concerted effort aimed at the specific media corporations involved and their controlling personnel.

- Catch your local media doing something "right" and bombard them with thanks and approval.
- Launch a communications campaign to corporations and their personnel demanding more responsible messages.
- Challenge television and radio licenses.
- Set up a "Person of the Year" or other reward system to thank your local programmers when they respond to community needs.

FAITH AND EXPECTATION

*"Faith is inseparable
from expectations.
Where there is real faith,
there is always expectation."*

—CATHERINE BOOTH, "THE ARMY MOTHER,"
CO-FOUNDER OF THE SALVATION ARMY

TARA WATSON

Using Her Crown to Help Kids

For Tara Watson, Miss Texas 2000, the "platform issue" for the Miss America Pageant was a very personal issue: AIDS awareness. A close friend of Tara's had died of the disease. The shock and grief had motivated Tara into action. Even before winning the Miss Texas crown she organized AIDS walks and tried to drive home to young people the message that AIDS isn't just a disease of society's fringes. "AIDS," she says, "does not discriminate."

The Miss Texas title gave Tara the platform she needed to take her message to thousands of schoolchildren across Texas. She used every opportunity, right up to her very last night as Miss Texas. The audience was riveted as Tara, just before crowning her successor, sang a song about a young woman dying because, through a one-night stand, "she let a stranger kill her hopes and her dreams." The lyrics never even mention "AIDS." But to everyone who heard Tara's performance, the message was clear.

FREE FROM THE PRESSURE OF OTHERS' IMAGES

"I have found that the more we are identified with Christ, the more freedom we have from the pressures of other people's images of us. How do you find your identity in Christ? You find it by allowing Him to show you your own heart, then by purifying your heart so that you become the same, inside and out."

NANCY CORBETT COLE, *THE UNIQUE WOMAN*

Nancy Corbett Cole (1924-2000) was an author and the co-founder, with her husband, Edwin Louis Cole, of Christian Men's Network. Her books include TAPESTRY OF LIFE: DEVOTIONS FOR THE UNIQUE WOMAN.

BEAUTY WITHOUT THE CONTEST

As Miss Missouri and a contestant in the Miss World USA pageant, I was focused on one thing: I wanted to win the crown. But as I began to compare myself with the other, more beautiful women on the stage beside me, insecurity and envy arose within. In my own mind, I didn't measure up. Of course, it didn't help that I was competing with Lynda Carter, a bona fide "Wonder Woman." (No wonder she won!)

When I speak to women's groups around the country I often ask, "Has anyone else here ever competed in a beauty contest?" I'll never forget the response of one dear woman who confessed, "EVERY DAY OF MY LIFE!"

In God's eyes we are beautiful, for God looks on the heart. My prayer for the sisterhood of Christ is that we develop more beautiful hearts. One great way to begin is to have the eyes of God as we gaze upon one another.

May we refuse to compare our individual gifts, and may we never look at life as a contest where someone else must lose if we are ever to win. May we each put race, nationality, economics, and all other manner of comparison aside, reach out to help one another, and know deep in our hearts the truth: In the only contest that really matters, God is the only judge. And in Christ Jesus, we are all beauties worthy to wear His crown.

☙

KALI SCHNIEDERS

Kali Schnieders is a professional speaker and the author of TRUFFLES FROM HEAVEN.

GOD'S BEAUTY PROGRAM

"Beloved, when you have put on
your beautiful garments of praise
(for no matter how homely you may be
to the natural eye, you are beautiful
to the Lord when you have put on
praise as a garment),
you are lifted above your own
'make-up' and 'disposition'
and swing far out
into the realm of the Spirit."

—AIMEE SEMPLE MCPHERSON,
THIS IS THAT, 1923

CELEBRATE!

*"Celebrating each new day
helps us develop the ability
to be grateful for all new moments
and for the God Who
is in each one."*

&

—KAREN BURTON MAINS

SOURCE: *With My Whole Heart* (Portland, OR: Multnomah Press, 1987)

FROM ISOLATION TO OUTREACH

At the age of fifteen I became a Christian—as far as I know, the first Christian woman in Malta. In Malta superstitious religion is not just part of the culture; it *is* the culture. Ten years of isolation and persecutions followed my accepting Christ.

Later, I married a wonderful Christian man. In 1983, we started the first Maltese Evangelical church, with 10 Maltese believers. Those 10 believers grew to 200. God then called us to help with a church in another, hostile part of the world–Libya.

In our 25 ministry trips in North Africa, we have seen women and children being devalued, neglected and treated as household items. My passion is to reach more North African women and equip them to advance the Kingdom of God in their countries. With the help of brothers and sisters in the U.S. and elsewhere we can make a difference.

❧

SYLVIA CARANUNA

CHANGING NEIGHBORHOODS AND NATIONS

IDA SCUDDER

Ida Scudder was, in 1899, one of the first women graduates of Cornell Medical College. Journeying to the other side of the world, she opened a single-bed clinic in Vellore, India. From that small beginning grew India's first medical school for women (it later began to admit men as well) and today's 1700-bed medical center in Vellore. The institution Dr. Scudder founded now houses 1,000 inpatients, sees 2,000 outpatients a day, conducts 43 operations and sees 16 births daily, and runs 22 clinics. The hospital also holds Bible classes and other ministry work.

SOURCE: Christian Medical College and Hospital Vellore

MARY KAY ASH

Opening Doors for Thousands

With her life savings of $5,000 and the help of her 20-year-old son, Richard Rogers, Mary Kay Ash launched Mary Kay Cosmetics in 1963. Her goal was to provide women with an unlimited opportunity for personal and financial success.

She used the Golden Rule as her guiding philosophy and encouraged employees and sales force members to prioritize their lives according to a simple but empowering motto: God first, family second, career third. As chairman emeritus of Mary Kay, Inc., this legendary businesswoman continues to inspire generations of women.

LET'S CELEBRATE UNSUNG HEROINES

Recently, while in Bosnia, I came across a book with the darkly ironic title *Love Your Neighbor: The Story of a War*. Written by a Bosnian war correspondent, it gives grim details of terrible devastation. I contrasted that *Love Your Neighbor* story with the one taught in Women of Global Action. We teach women how to care and share their faith with their neighbors, building eternal relationships.

God is using women worldwide to build His kingdom— women who truly love their neighbors in real and practical ways, like reaching out to HIV/AIDS sufferers and orphans in Africa. Sometimes it is at great cost. This does not deter them, it motivates them! I am encouraged to see women who carry the cross daily for Christ.

Let's celebrate how an awesome God is using the hundreds of thousands of unsung heroines to make a kingdom difference in this world. Although we will never know many of their names or know of their significant contributions to the Kingdom, I want to always share celebrating their contributions.

꒕

EMILY VOORHIES

Emily Voorhies is executive director of Women of Global Action. She has been in international ministry for more than 20 years and has lived in Sweden, Kenya, and Zimbabwe for thirteen.

BRAVING THE VIOLENCE, LOVING THE PEOPLE

After one too many forays into a certain village, I found myself surrounded by a mob of angry, militant Muslims. They began to spit and throw stones at the Bible students and me.

"Why do you keep coming back?" the constable who took us into protective custody questioned us. He knew we knew that Christians were unwelcome in Muslim villages—considered a form of pollution.

"We want to tell the people how much God loves them," I answered in a calm voice. "I'll be OK. I have people in the United States praying for me."

At the mention of the United States, the constable became alarmed. What if my praying friends heard that we had been martyred in his village? An act of violence against Christians could start an international incident! He knew he could not let the mob who wanted to kill me have their way—regardless of how troublesome I was.

The constable dispersed the crowd and sent us on our way —this time.

℘

WATI

Wati is the pseudonym of a woman who ministers in a Muslim area, one of countless women risking everything for the gospel in countries around the world.

THE NEW TRADITIONAL WOMAN

Who is the New Traditional Woman? She is a mother of the citizens of the 21st century. It is she who will more than anyone else transmit civilization and humanity to future generations, and by her response to the challenges of life, determine whether America will be a strong, virtuous nation.

The New Traditional Woman is not the vicious cartoon that the feminist movement has made of wives and mothers. The New Traditional Woman is not the syrupy caricature that Hollywood of the 1950's beamed into our living rooms. She is new, because she is of the current era, with all its pressures and fast pace and rapid change. She is traditional because, in the face of unremitting cultural change, she is oriented around the eternal truths of faith and family. Her values are timeless and true to human nature.

⁊

CONNAUGHT MARSHNER

Excerpt from Connaught C. Marshner, THE NEW TRADITIONAL WOMAN
(Free Congress Research and Education Foundation, 1982)

AT THE FRONT LINES IN INDONESIA

As a doctor, I have seen tragic, bloody war waged by Jihad warriors in Ambon and Maluku. My eyes have watched as homes and churches went up in flames. Even the seminary where I work was targeted for destruction. Innocent men, women and children have been slaughtered, while many others are left homeless, all belongings only memories.

Remaining refugees are being ministered to by our outreach. Local Christians and seminary students are providing food, medicines and school supplies. Many have come to Christ as God's people reach out in love, in partnership with the Body of Christ.

℘

DR. ERIANA

Dr. Eriana is the Director of Wholistic Ministries, Evangelical Theological Seminary of Indonesia.

CHARACTER CHOICES DETERMINE THE JOURNEY

In 20 years as a broadcast newswoman, it was electrifying to see famous people and witness historical events from a front-row perspective. Being in the middle of everything was the best—and the worst—thing about my job. No one really wants a front-row seat at the scene of a murder or a child sexual abuse trial. What's more, I agreed with the people who criticize the lack of substance and relevance on most newscasts. Yet there I was every day.

I asked God to let certain people "see the light," asked for promotion to a new position, for relief from the isolation of difficult hours. Then one day I realized I wasn't praying the right prayer. The right prayer was for personal change instead of asking for the world to change.

It's amazing how many people continue to do the same things while expecting different results. Now I work to help others see how every decision made is a character choice that will affect their future. Character choices determine the journey for us.

%

ANITA VANETTI

Former TV reporter and anchorwoman Anita Vanetti is a consultant specializing in character and confidence training for businesspersons, public speakers, actors and others.

ANNEKE COMPANJEN

Encountering Women, Sharing Hope

Anneke Companjen has given a voice to women throughout the persecuted church in her recent book, *Hidden Sorrow, Lasting Joy*. In the book, already published in six languages, Anneke reveals the stories of 20 women who have suffered because they, with their husbands, chose to follow Christ despite opposition and danger. The wife of Johan Companjen, president of Open Doors International, Anneke continues to travel to restricted countries to meet with and minister to these courageous women with stories still untold.

PEACE-MAKERS, NOT POWER-SEEKERS

The answer to women's needs today will not be found in dividing into two emotionally charged camps, glaring at each other, finding fault and placing blame. What we need are peace-makers, not power-seekers. The tension of division is destructive.

I believe that God wants to raise up today an army of women who will find their identity in Him. He does not seek to put down, but rather to build up. He can replace all the "how to" handbooks with the "Maker's manual"—the Bible, whose truths are timeless. I believe that He will raise up "another voice" for women, and that other voice will be that of all those special women who will heed His call to come and "follow Him."

Yes, there is a persistent problem women sense today, one that seems to have no name. Ah, but I have discovered its name. Its name is hunger, spiritual hunger. It is the cause of the gnawing, yearning unrest in the heart of today's woman. And only He, our Lord Jesus Christ, can satisfy that spiritual hunger. Saint Augustine said it centuries ago: "Thou hast created us for thyself, and our heart cannot be quieted till it may find repose in thee."

ℒ

DEE JEPSEN, *WOMEN: BEYOND EQUAL RIGHTS*
(WORD PUBLISHING, WACO, TEXAS, 1984)

Dee Jepsen is president of Enough is Enough. A vocal anti-pornography activist, she is working for passage of "The Protection of Children from Computer Pornography Act."

PRAYER FOR EVERY SCHOOL, EVERY CHILD

Mothers worry if what their children learn in the classroom undermines their family values. Add to that the fear of violence. In 1960 the top offenses in public schools included chewing gum, running in the halls, wearing improper clothing, making noise, not putting paper in wastebaskets, and getting out of turn in line. Top offenses in public schools today include rape, robbery, assault, personal theft, burglary, drug abuse, arson, bombings, alcohol abuse, carrying of weapons, absenteeism, vandalism, murder, extortion, and gang warfare, to name only a few.

The immediate vision of Moms In Touch International is for mothers to pray for every school in the United States by the end of the year 2003. Our ultimate goal is to see every child prayed for around the world.

❧

SHARON ARRINGTON

Sharon Arrington is Southwest regional coordinator of Moms in Touch International. MITI prayer groups meet for an hour each week to pray for their children and their schools, teachers, and administrators.

FROM ORPHANAGE TO INTERNATIONAL MINISTRY

As an infant I was placed in the New York Foundling Home and later raised as a foster child. I founded Dare to Dream Children's Foundation to help children living in shelters, foster homes, and orphanages. As a choreographer and writer, I challenge young people to "dare to dream!" and discover a passion for life.

JAN TENNYSON

Jan Tennyson is founder and director of Dare to Dream Children's Foundation, based in Dallas, Texas. The foundation ministers throughout the world to youth in tragic and seemingly hopeless situations.

AWAKENING THE MOMMA BEAR CONSTITUENCY

We all know what happens when a predator threatens a cub bear. The momma bear rises up to protect her offspring. I feel led to encourage what I call the "Momma Bear constituency."

Today, Momma Bears throughout this nation need to understand the serious dangers facing their children. We need to raise up an army of women who will stand for righteousness. We need prayer warriors who will lift up our government leaders. We also need activist Momma Bears at the local and state level who will defend their children from immorality and sexual seduction.

Twelve brave librarians in Minneapolis won a recent victory over Internet pornography in their libraries. The women sued the library system because it permitted unfiltered access to pornography on all library computers. As a result, pornography-addicted men took over most of the computers and left printouts of child pornography, bestiality, and other obscene photos near the terminals. These librarians feared for their personal safety and were offended by having to view obscene pictures every day. They filed a complaint with the Equal Employment Opportunity Commission (EEOC) saying the library system was forcing them to work in a "hostile environment." They felt sexually harassed and they were concerned that children were being exposed to pornography. The EEOC sided with them in May 2001.

These brave women took a stand against a social evil that had invaded their libraries. They did so on behalf of their own personal safety—and the safety of the children who were exposed to pornography. These Momma Bears made a difference. So can you.

The book of James says that faith without works is dead. We must be willing to take a stand for righteousness in our culture. We cannot allow evil to be called good and good to be called evil. Many times an attitude of indifference pervades our churches today. There is a feeling that efforts to oppose pornography are "political" efforts that do not deserve our attention. These are moral issues—and Christians must be concerned with morality. It is our duty to oppose immorality in our culture. We are to be a restraining force against the powers that are seeking to limit the preaching and teaching of the glorious gospel of the Lord Jesus Christ.

If evil laws, evil teaching in schools, and evil on TV and in movies are not restrained, we will lose many of our children to evil ways. Evangelism will be much more difficult. It may become impossible to preach against sin. It is said we are in a "post-Christian era." Why? Because the church has been indifferent to its duty. It has failed to keep the heritage from our founding fathers to be involved in all areas of life—including politics and social change.

Jesus told us in Matthew 5:13-16: "You are the salt of the earth. But if the salt loses its saltiness, how can it be made salty again? It is no longer good for anything, except to be thrown out and trampled by men. You are the light of the world. A city on a hill cannot be hidden. Neither do people light a lamp and put it under a bowl. Instead, they put it on its stand, and it gives light to everyone in the house. In the same way, let your light shine before men, that they may see your good deeds and praise your Father in heaven." These are words to the Momma Bears.

Each day we need to stake a claim for our children, our families, our schools and our government. We need to speak boldly and without fear at school board meetings, at the town hall, and even in the halls of Congress. We need to reclaim all of these for Jesus Christ. Where we live must be where we take this stand.

~

ANDREA LAFFERTY

As executive director of the Traditional Values Coalition, Andrea Lafferty lobbies in behalf of over 43,000 churches, emphasizing issues such as education, family tax relief, pornography, the right to life, and religious freedom.

A CONGRESSMAN PAYS TRIBUTE TO A MORAL LEADER

Andrea Aulbert, a woman whose life, though brief, was one of impressive accomplishment. Andrea served as the director of legislative and legal affairs for Concerned Women of America until her death on July 2, 2000, at the age of 33. Andrea spent her life in service to others, from her student days as a camp counselor, to her advocacy on behalf of persecuted Christians in China and other countries, to her tireless efforts in her professional career in support of moral renewal and the sanctity of human life. The good that she did in her short life will be felt for years to come by thousands of people who never knew her at all. That is the definition of a true American hero, Andrea Aulbert.

℀

REP. TOM COBURN (R-OKLA.),
TO THE U.S. HOUSE OF REPRESENTATIVES

Excerpted from Mr. Coburn's remarks on the floor of the House, October 30, 2000.

PUTTING COMPASSION INTO ACTION

Having become a Christian in my 30's, sharing Christ became my major thrust in life. The result is that I have traveled to over 25 countries in church planting, showing the *Jesus* film, and knocking on doors. I saw the effects of poverty on the world. My heart became burdened for the poor.

The Dallas chapter of Women of Vision was birthed in 1995 when I enlisted friends to help. Women with diverse talents used their God-given trait of compassion to accomplish great things for the Lord, greater than a single person could do alone. Women of Vision is a hands-on fundraising program associated with World Vision, one of the largest Christian humanitarian organizations in the world.

Our first project: Bosnia. Our teams have gone into that country four times in the past five years. Traumatized Bosnian children, women who have lost everything, including husbands, brothers, fathers, and uncles receive our outstretched hands. Grateful for the small amounts of money we lend them, Bosnians start little businesses that generate incomes.

In Mexico City, teams are sent to reclaim the lives of street children. To help break the generational cycle of poverty, we work in microenterprise development, giving small loans to women in the barrios.

In Dallas, volunteers have worked with an inner-city school for six years. This school is in one of the most crime-ridden areas of our city. Aftercare programs for women coming out of prison is another arena where so much love and understanding are needed

and given by volunteers. Our newest project is a women's shelter in the city. Women of Vision provides many opportunities for women to carry out the mandate to help the poor.

ANNE MILLER

Anne Miller serves on the Board of Directors for World Vision and is wife of Interstate Batteries Chairman, Norm Miller.

LESLEE UNRUH

Inviting Young People into Self-Respect and Purity

Speaking to teen groups, writing columns for the nation's newspapers, and appearing on everything from the *Oprah Winfrey Show* to James Dobson's *Focus on the Family* radio program, Leslee J. Unruh addresses teens' "hot-button" topics: sexuality, self-respect, and building relationships. The mother of five and grandmother of two, she uses humor, straight talk and personal experience to make a serious message inviting for its audience.

Leslee is the founder and president of the National Abstinence Clearinghouse, a resource center that distributes information on sexual abstinence and provides training to educators and parents. And she is also founder and president of a pregnancy care center that sees 5,000 clients a year. She lives with her husband in Sioux Falls, South Dakota.

A VISION FOR THE BIBLICAL TRUTH OF EQUALITY

On Bastille Day we wore French costumes, ate snails, and sang the Marseillaise. On other occasions our family ate stuffed grape leaves, humus, and an assortment of eggplant and lamb dishes as part of our Lebanese heritage. My mother was born in France, my father in Lebanon. French, Arabic, and English were spoken in our home. My sister and I juggled several languages and cultures throughout our childhood. The significance of religious icons was discussed as we remembered the Christian heritage of our family in Lebanon. Though both my parents were culturally Christian, I came to a deep personal faith in high school through close friends.

Apologetics, theology and church history became my passions in college and seminary. My passion for church history and women's contributions in eras past, led me to begin a research project on the Welsh revivalists. Jessie Penn-Lewis, whose gifts were used by God to bring revival and the Gospel to many people around the world, became the topic of my dissertation.

Women rise to the highest heights God has created for them when the biblical truth of equality is embraced and properly interpreted. I envision a future where women all over the world will exercise all their gifts to God's glory with the full support of the Christian community.

&

MIMI HADDAD

Mimi Haddad is President of Minneapolis-based Christians for Biblical Equality.

LEADERSHIP PROFILE
BARBARA VON DER HEYDT ELLIOTT

"The longer I walk with Him, the more I let go of the old self and try to make myself available for what He is doing."

After a successful career as a PBS reporter and international correspondent, Barbara von der Heydt Elliott stopped to wonder if she had produced anything of lasting significance. Coming up with a short list, she prayed. The one-word answer was "refugees." In the summer of 1989, she saw a huge stream of 300,000 people pouring in through the hole in the Iron Curtain between Hungary and West Germany. What her heart said was not "somebody" should care for those people but that *she* should.

Barbara had graduated from Ohio Wesleyan University, and pursued graduate studies at George Washington University and St. Thomas University. She then served the Heritage Foundation, and was appointed to the White House Office of Public Liaison, before moving to Europe where she covered economic and political news as a television correspondent.

Hearing God call her to "refugees," Barbara found those who were within driving distance of where she lived in Cologne, and took them clothes, pots, pans and blankets. She then helped them find jobs, doctors, places to live and even tutors for their children. From her experiences, she wrote a book entitled *Candles Behind the Wall.*

In 1997, Barbara returned to the U.S. and started the "Center for Renewal," a resource center for faith-based entrepreneurs working to renew the inner cities of America. A writer and speaker, Barbara champions the cause nationwide for faith-based and community initiatives.

PRAY GLOBALLY...

FOR AN END TO DOMESTIC VIOLENCE WORLDWIDE

In a study of British women, up to 25% reported having experienced physical abuse at the hands of an intimate partner. Violence was associated with increased rates of miscarriage, premature birth, low birth weight, and fetal injury, including fetal death.

Canadian women with a violent father-in-law are reported at three times the risk for spousal abuse as Canadian women with a non-violent father-in-law. One in four women in Latin America is a victim of physical abuse. In Romania, 29% of women between ages 15 and 55 who sought treatment at the Bucharest Forensic Hospital had been beaten by an intimate partner. Of these, 87% had been assaulted by an instrument that pierced the skin.

In India and other parts of Asia, three out of four women reported some form of physical abuse. One of every four South African women is assaulted domestically. In Peru 49% and in the Gaza Strip 38% of all women are assaulted in their homes.

Children who watch the victimization of their mothers are five times more likely to exhibit serious behavioral problems than other children.

- Pray that Christians will no longer ignore this problem.
- Pray that Christians will not abdicate responsibility toward this tragedy to oppressive governments and to activist non-Christian groups.
- Pray for dramatic, positive changes for those in abusive domestic relationships.

SUBMITTING TO GOD, NOT TO ABUSE

Intelligent. Competent. Assured. These words paint the picture of an attractive, energetic young woman whom I had known casually for over ten years. But when I received word that, at the hands of her husband, she had been a victim of repeated violence, my first thought was, *How could this be?*

She had met her husband at a respected seminary. However, after marriage, her confidence decreased and her fear increased. No one knew she was being abused.

But how could she tell anyone? She wanted to protect the image of her little family. Surely if she "tried hard enough" he would stop—typically that's what abused women think. But not so. Now he was divorcing her for another woman, and they were in the midst of a custody battle over their two young sons. The judge ruled that until a decision was made as to which parent would have custodial care, this arrangement was to be followed: The children were to stay in the home, and each parent would rotate in and out every other week. So every other week for about a year and a half, when her husband was with the kids she stayed in my home.

During one of our many late-night talks I asked if she had any pictures to prove to the judge that her husband was an untrustworthy, violent man. She went to the guest bedroom and returned with pictures of herself—police photographs that showed her head severely bruised and swollen. I was stunned. I hadn't expected such graphic pictures.

When I gave her our ministry's material on wife abuse, titled *Wife Abuse: Assault on a Woman's Worth*, she quickly identified with the "scripture twisting." This simply means that most wife batterers are adept at manipulating their wives with the verse, "Wives, submit to your husbands." Naturally, they fail to apply to themselves all the verses against violence. After an incident of wife abuse, too many women hear foolish statements like *What did you do to cause it?* — as though his sin of violence is her fault. (Now she is being doubly victimized.)

No wonder many women who suffer abuse are disheartened, confused and distressed. They wonder, *Must I really suffer at the angry hands of someone who has sworn to cherish and protect me?* God's answer is no. Specifically, the Bible says, "Do not associate with any one easily angered." (Proverbs 22:24) It is biblical for victims of violence to separate themselves from the victimizer.

What about victims who are made to feel guilty because they reported the abuse to the police? They are bearing the weight of false guilt. The Bible says, "A hot tempered man must pay the penalty. If you rescue him, you will have to do it again." (Proverbs 19:19)

But what if a wife assumes she must submit to whatever her husband inflicts upon her? If she truly wants to be biblical, she must look at the whole counsel of God. Then she will see there is a hierarchy of submission. First Peter 2 presents that we are to submit to the civil authorities. Since domestic violence is against the law, she should not submit to that which is against the law. In truth, she should report such incidents with the prayer that a legal consequence of police intervention and possible jail time would motivate her husband to get the help he needs.

Above all, the highest form of submission is to God. Acts 5:29 says, "We must obey God rather than man." So what does God say? "Bring to an end your violence and make the righteous secure." (Psalm 7:9) Sometimes a wife must say no to a husband so that she can say yes to God.

If any of us submit to or tacitly condone ungodly abuse, we are doing what most officers did in Nazi Germany. In spite of the human atrocities, many Germans took the position, "I had no choice—I had to submit." No, a wife should never be encouraged to submit to that which is against the Law of God.

One in three women worldwide is a victim of domestic violence. One in three! So where is God amidst such ungodly suffering? He is not only with those who suffer, but He also has provided a way of deliverance through His Word. The joy of hope and healing is available to any who seek it. And we should be bearers of God's message of freedom—freedom for women who feel emotionally and physically imprisoned. The Bible says,

> *"Then you will know the truth,*
> *and the truth will set you free."*
> *(John 8:32)*

So, what happened to my friend who had been repeatedly abused? After two years, she was awarded custody of her children. Second, the judge admitted that, in retrospect, his better judgment would have been to assign only one parent custodial care until a permanent decision was made. And last, my friend's ex-husband served no time in jail and received no sentencing for his abuse.

℔

JUNE HUNT

June Hunt is founder of Hope for the Heart and hosts the live radio counseling program, HOPE IN THE NIGHT.

ACT LOCALLY...

ON THE PROBLEMS OF VIOLENCE IN THE HOME

You lock your doors at night, you check behind the seat before driving home, have a friend walk you to the car when it's dark, install a burglar alarm, don't give rides to strangers, and you don't stroll down eerie alleys.

Yet one third of all female homicide victims are killed by their husbands, boyfriends or ex-boyfriends (between 2,000 and 4,000 victims annually in the U.S.). Almost six times as many women are assaulted by those they know as opposed to attacked by strangers. As many as one in three women will be assaulted by a domestic partner in her lifetime—equaling four million every year. Animal shelters are more prevalent in America than shelters for women.

According to statistics, police are more likely to respond within five minutes if the offender is a stranger than if the offender is known to the victim. One third of the misdemeanor assaults would be considered felonies if perpetrated by a stranger.

- Work with your local police to develop a policy toward spousal abuse.
- Offer your services to your local church to create a resource for abuse victims, and for perpetrators who want to change.
- Launch an education program in your local high schools and churches about domestic abuse.
- Start a shelter for abused women and children.

FORGIVENESS BROUGHT FREEDOM

I have been hurt in life to a very deep degree. I was abused, abandoned, rejected, blamed, lied about, misunderstood and betrayed by family and friends. I was abused sexually, verbally, emotionally, and mentally, and I allowed Satan to fill my heart with hatred for those who hurt me. But when I began to learn about love, I moved from hatred to bitterness, then to mild resentment, and finally to freedom, which comes only through forgiveness ... Love includes forgiveness, and forgiveness requires letting go of the past.

JOYCE MEYER, *REDUCE ME TO LOVE*
(HARRISON HOUSE, TULSA, OKLAHOMA, 2000)

Joyce Meyer's ministry is internationally known through her conferences and her Life in the Word television program.

PRAY GLOBALLY...

ABOUT THE RISE OF DOMESTIC VIOLENCE WITHIN OUR CHURCHES

The United States-based Christian Reformed Church conducted a survey among a random sample of 1,000 adult members attending their churches. Of the 643 responses, 28% had experienced at least one form of abuse. For 12% it was physical abuse, 13% sexual abuse, and 19% emotional abuse. Converting that study to actual numbers, the church estimated that 48,000 to 62,000 Christian Reformed Church members have experienced physical, sexual, or emotional abuse.

If left unaddressed, these facts can lead to misconceptions and irresponsible assumptions by secular and even church-affiliated advocacy groups. It has been alleged that biblical principles cause men to be violent toward their wives or at least provide fertile soil for men's misuse of power within their families. Some argue that since the church is part of the problem, it cannot be part of the solution.

- Pray for men's groups and Christian role models to take a firm stand against abuse.
- Pray that the truth of God's Word will prevail, correcting misconceptions of biblical principles.
- Pray for older Christian women to rise up and teach the younger to understand whom they must listen to as authority figures and whom they must shun.

USING OUR VOICES AND OUR HANDS FOR THE OPPRESSED

To expose the atrocity of child prostitution and raise the plight of street children, I have addressed the United Nations Human Rights Commission in Geneva, Switzerland, on five occasions since 1992. I helped launch the opening of "Jubilee House" outside of Bombay, India, as a shelter for the daughters of prostitutes. Jubilee Campaign promotes the human rights and religious liberty of ethnic and religious minorities in countries that imprison, terrorize, or otherwise oppress them.

Jubilee Campaign advocates the release of prisoners of conscience and the change of laws as necessary to affect these purposes. We launched a campaign in which members of the House and Senate were asked to lobby governments in countries where child atrocities occur, including Brazil, Guatemala, India, the Philippines, and Burma.

Through fact-finding missions to Islamabad and Lahore, Pakistan, I have led international delegations of activists concerned about the long-term incarceration and prevalent abuse of Christian prisoners of conscience.

Jubilee Campaign USA led a congressional fact-finding mission to Indonesia to gain first-hand information concerning the persecution of Christians in the Maluku or Spice Islands. Additional fact-finding trips in which I have participated have included Nepal, India, the Philippines, and the Thai-Burma border areas.

♀

ANNE J. BUWALDA

Anne has led dangerous, and still secret, rescue missions to escort persecuted believers to safe haven. She founded the law firm, Just Law International, to focus on immigration law and asylum and refugee cases.

OUT OF SLAVERY, SALVATION

"Twas mercy brought me
from my Pagan land,
Taught my benighted soul
to understand
That there's a God,
that there's a Saviour too:
Once I redemption
neither sought nor knew."

—PHILLIS WHEATLEY

Phillis Wheatley (1753-1784) was brought from Africa to Boston in 1761, when she was six years old. As a slave, she was educated through her mistress in English and Latin. Her first poem was published in 1767, and a volume of poems was published in 1773. She was highly respected as a writer and poetess throughout her lifetime.

CHANGING NEIGHBORHOODS AND NATIONS

HARRIET BEECHER STOWE

"A day of grace is yet held out to us. Both North and South have been guilty before God; and the Christian church has a heavy account to answer. Not by combining together, to protect injustice and cruelty, and making a common capital of sin, is this Union to be saved, but by repentance, justice and mercy."

HARRIET BEECHER STOWE, *UNCLE TOM'S CABIN*

Powerful words ran in the family. The father of Harriet Beecher Stowe (1811-1896), Lyman Beecher, was a New England minister, and her brother, Henry Ward Beecher was one of the most prominent preachers of the 19th century. But the power of her words may have surpassed them both. Harriet's 1852 novel UNCLE TOM'S CABIN *greatly fueled the abolitionist movement, prompting President Abraham Lincoln's famous greeting: "So you're the little lady who started the big war."*

ELIZABETH MITTLSTAEDT

Starting a European Magazine for Ministry

Before her conversion to Christ, Elizabeth Mittlstaedt was a dedicated Communist. Even then she dreamed of someday using her gift of writing. She originally thought she would use her government college scholarship to enhance her skills to write Communist materials. Meeting Christ changed those plans for her life, and cost her the scholarship. However, Elizabeth knew God was in control.

God provided three years in the Swiss Bible School after a visit with missionary Olga Olson. During college vacations, she helped Swedish missionaries slip into Romania, Hungary, and Yugoslavia, holding children's camps, as well as encountering life-threatening events. Bible school brought her Ditmar Mittlstaedt, a German student from Canada, who became her husband. Together they pastored in America, then followed Ditmar's missionary call to Germany. There God revealed that He desired a "magazine for ministry."

Elizabeth and Ditmar used household money and some mission funds for the first issue of *Lydia*. For the third issue, a total of ten thousand copies were printed, but she wasn't satisfied to stop there, saying, "God, it would be so nice if you put one more zero at the back." By the end of its tenth year *Lydia* had a circulation of more than 90,000 in Germany alone and was moving toward the goal of distribution in other nations. Her German readers made it possible to begin sending *Lydia* into Romania, and now *Lydia* ministers across the European continent.

Adapted from Lorry Lutz, WOMEN AS RISK TAKERS FOR GOD *(Baker Books, Grand Rapids, Michigan, 1997)*

WE MUST BE FILLED

"What can the glove do? The glove can do nothing. Oh, but if my hand is in the glove, it can do many things ... cook, play the piano, write. Well, you say that is not the glove, that is the hand in the glove that does it. Yes, that is so. I tell you that we are nothing but gloves. The hand in the glove is the Holy Spirit of God. Can the glove do something if it is very near the hand? No! The glove must be filled with the hand to do the work. That is exactly the same for us; we must be filled with the Holy Spirit to do the work God has for us to do."

CORRIE TEN BOOM

The legacy of minister and concentration camp survivor Corrie ten Boom (1893-1983) continues to encourage and inspire countless Christians around the world.

HE DOES FULFILL OUR DESIRES

At 17, the acting bug bit, and some time later I surrendered my life to God. When I gave a performance as Corrie ten Boom, women's hearts were touched, and that began a ministry of sharing wonderful lives of the past with beautiful women of the present.

Corrie was an ordinary woman who believed God and that He would lead her to do extraordinary work for Him. Like Corrie, I knew God could do miracles if He could put joy in my depressed spirit. I believed and vowed to follow Him. God has taken an ordinary woman and used me to bring to life on stage heroines of days gone by. He does fulfill the desires of our hearts if we commit our ways unto him.

℘

EVELYN HINDS

Evelyn Hinds is an actress who portrays historical figures such as Corrie ten Boom and Laura Ingalls Wilder.

HEALING BROKEN HEARTS ONE AT A TIME

The Apostle John was inspired to communicate in finite words the infinite Word made flesh, the Source and sustenance of all life. He was successful not because he was a clever wordsmith, but because he was aware of his real assignment: to bear witness to a Truth he knew and loved.

Nothing less is being asked of us today. We are being "called by name" to communicate the truth about the dignity of human life. The humanity being subjected to the cruelest and most degrading forms of abuse and injustice reminds us to recognize this challenge. We can no longer dodge the question: Why have we fallen so far short of forming a civilization worthy of the description "a culture of life?" Why would any civilized society tolerate the miserable, wretched conditions that constitute a culture of death over those that protect, defend, and nurture life?

No longer can we shift the responsibility for any solution into the hands of those over whom we have little or no control. It's time to fix our gaze where our own deepest attitudes are formed. This is where, as the Greeks would say, a genuine *metanoya* or profound change must first take place. Genuine renewal is needed within ourselves if we are to be empowered to help build a culture of life.

We might begin by asking, "When did I neglect to 'love my neighbor as myself' by turning a deaf ear to the cries of the oppressed, the lonely, the confused? When did I refuse to forgive, much less love, my enemy, preferring to hold on to grudges and nurse old wounds?"

The greatest communicator left the pattern to show us how to improve. Not only did our Lord express His love through concrete, tangible actions, but He preferred to deliver His message to one soul at a time. When He cured the leper, forgave the sinner, consoled the widow, raised the dead, made the lame to walk and the blind to see, He reached out and touched one broken, hurting person at a time, healing their wounds—one life at a time.

This awareness caused my professional life to take a sharp detour from the grandeur of an executive suite in midtown Manhattan to a modest office for an international charity. While it took the personal anguish of a mid-trimester miscarriage for me to grasp the horror of prenatal death, it has taken the life-saving activity of the Nurturing Network to teach me the value of translating my reverence for all human life into concrete action.

The thousands of "Mary Magdalenes" that Nurturing Network serves confirm that binding deep wounds and healing broken hearts is an intimate experience. There is no effective substitute for private, personal, time-intensive conversations that relate the best message of all: "You are a beloved child of God. No matter what mistake you may have made or sin you may have committed, you are valuable and precious in God's sight."

&

MARY CUNNINGHAM AGEE

Mary Cunningham Agee is founder and executive director of the Nurturing Network, an organization that provides a positive alternative to abortion. Voted by WORLD ALMANAC *as one of "The 25 Most Influential Women in America," she is the author of a best-selling autobiography,* POWERPLAY.

LEADERSHIP PROFILE

JUDY MBUGUA

Carrying a Light in Africa and Beyond

"It is a challenge to Christians to lessen the tension between sexes, to loosen chains that have bound women in the area of ministry and simply to recognize their potential," says Judy Mbugua. "Working together in harmony will bring glory to God."

Judy grew up in an African village with a love for God so intense that as a 7-year old she asked to be lifted onto a high table in order to give her testimony. In 1989, she was asked to start a women's branch of the Association Of Evangelicals in Africa. Today, Pan African Christian Women's Association has chapters in more than 30 African nations, and Judy travels the world to help mobilize and empower women.

Among the objectives of Pan African Christian Women's Association are to assert the true dignity of women as found in God's Word; to inject into African society biblical morals and values through the continent's women; to educate women in matters of justice, equity, and socio-economic development; and to foster cooperation among women's ministries in Africa.

Adapted from Lorry Lutz, WOMEN AS RISK TAKERS FOR GOD *(Baker Books, Grand Rapids, Michigan, 1997)*

My "Evolution" As A Creationist

The evolutionary interpretation of science and natural history was taught as "gospel" in my formative years. It wasn't until I received my degree and worked for two years in cancer research that I realized it contradicted with the Bible. Then, the man I married challenged my views of the scientific accuracy and general credibility of Scripture, which launched me into an intense personal study of the Bible and creation science. It was during this period that Jesus Christ became my Lord and Master. The Institute for Creation Research provided abundant information, convincing me of the biblical interpretation of science and natural history. The miraculous release from that great intellectual and emotional burden I had carried was a tremendous feeling. I realized my Bible was fully reliable down to the last word, jot and tittle. Studying my Bible and creation science became my passion.

God began to provide opportunities for me to share creation science with others. While I had no "game plan" of my own, God propelled me into a national ministry. My joy now is to "destroy speculations and every lofty thing raised up against the knowledge of God." The truth of creation and how it all fits together in history empowers individuals to discern the error of evolutionary influences in science, history, society, and other areas it has infiltrated.

ℒ

Catie Frates

Trained as a microbiologist, Catie Frates has worked in cancer research, taught high school science, and lectured on creation science. She is affiliated with Censored Science, a creation science ministry.

SOURCE: *Salt and Light Solutions*, Coral Ridge Ministries, Fort Lauderdale, Florida.

A COUNTER-CULTURAL COMMUNITY CALLED CHURCH

Undeniably female, unapologetically black, unashamedly Christian — that's my heritage. God has created His counter-cultural community called Church that is diverse in participants, but unified in participation.

As the first African American female ordained as an elder in the West Michigan Annual Conference, God has opened many doors for me. Providing models and encouragement for both male and female members of the Asbury seminary community, my goal is to develop a scriptural theology of women in ministry, and the Center for American Cultural Diversity is one of my projects.

JOY MOORE

Joy Moore is a director of the United Methodist General Commission on Church Unity and Inter-Religious Concerns.

GOD'S WORD
IN THE NATION'S SCHOOLS

"My goal is to have
a Bible course curriculum,
as an elective,
in the public high schools nationwide."

≈

—ELIZABETH RIDENOUR

Elizabeth Ridenour is founder and president of the National Council on
Bible Curriculum in Public Schools. She is a certified paralegal, an asso-
ciate member of the National Foundation for Women Legislators, and a
member for the Council for National Policy.

FACING A WRENCHING DECISION

For over 30 years, Africa invaded my heart. The first year, Africa engrafted herself into my soul, and God's faithfulness to His Word was engrafted into my spirit forever. Our family arrived at the remote, desolate town of Rahama in Northern Nigeria, ready to spread the Gospel. "Home" was an old two-story mud and thatched-roof house, with a "lean-to" for a kitchen, lacking only running water and electricity.

We enrolled 14-year-old Paul Jr. in boarding school 50 miles away. The first Easter break from boarding school brought the somber news that he had contracted a rare tropical disease and that he was unresponsive to all available treatments. Nearing the birth of our third child, Michael, we faced the heartbreak of uprooting Paul Jr's life again, sending him back to America.

As a family, we shared Michael's birth joyfully, and I hid the heaviness of my heart from the children. Alone in that hospital room, I had to face the question, could I give up my oldest son and let him live in California with the gracious couple who had offered to raise him as their own? What would be the emotional cost upon his life? Every breath felt like it was my last one. My heart could not bear more pain, yet I knew the others needed me. This is the only way I have been able to explain what took place: One second I couldn't breathe for pain; the next second was total peace. It had to be INSTANT GRACE!

My husband could not believe my peace, waving good-bye to the plane carrying my son thousands of miles away. The secret promise that God gave to me in that hospital room was 2 Timothy

1:12: "For I know whom I have believed, and am persuaded that He is able to keep that which I have committed unto Him against that day."

Eventually, Paul Jr. received treatment for the disease and gradually healed. Our family held reunions when we returned from the mission field, and we were reunited as a family when we returned from Africa permanently.

&

HELEN BRUTON

Helen, with her husband, the Rev. J. Paul Bruton, gave over 30 years to the continent of Africa. They began in 1948 in French Togo, then pioneered Bible schools and churches in West Africa, East Africa, as well as the first mission compound in Arusha, Tanzania, a key outpost on the route to Mount Kilimanjaro.

KEPT IN THE FAMILY

My calling to ministry is an exciting journey of obedience to God. "He which hath begun a good work in you will perform it until the day of Jesus Christ." (Phil 1:6) I believe in this promise, that life is a growing experience in the love of Jesus Christ and loving service to Him.

Born into a Canadian military family, I caught a global perspective on life as the family moved throughout Canada and Europe. My Christian parents were faithful witnesses to the joys of service to family and community and I accepted the Lord at an early age. The Salvation Army became my place of worship, as my parents and grandparents before me. My sense of calling to ministry was a driving motivation in my late teens. After college I taught school for three years in Canada then trained as a Salvation Army officer. I met my husband, Ed, while in training and together we have served for twenty-five years as corps officers in various headquarters appointments and U.S. National Headquarters. Throughout our officership, our two daughters have ministered alongside. God begins a "good work" in us and He is faithful in all things to perform it.

$\mathcal{L}$

CAROLYNNE CHUNG

Major Carolynne Chung is now stationed in London, England, training resources and conferences for lay leaders within the Adult and Family Ministries throughout the UK.

TRUE PEACE

As she received the Nobel Peace Prize,
she was asked,
"What can we do to promote world peace?"
Mother Teresa replied,
"Go home and love your family."

SOURCE: The Almanac of the Christian World.

JUST LOVE THEM, AND KEEP COOKING

In bringing up my children, I didn't make any difference between them. They were all brought up the same way. I supported Junior (A.C.) in his choices. I have been there for him, but I didn't treat the other kids different.

When he started getting famous, I would always tell Junior, "Remember where you came from." Today he's a humble man. God opened up doors for Junior, and he opened up doors for the family. But he's nobody's pillow. He likes helping people, but he wants others to get up and help themselves as well.

Junior comes back to town and stays with us. The other kids say, "Yeah, Junior is coming," because they see me start cooking. But that's just a gentle teasing because they know that if they lived out of town and came home, I'd do the same for them.

A mother can bring up her children, but they have their own ideas. We just love them and back them, and keep cooking.

LEOLA GREEN

Leola Green is the mother of NBA "Ironman" basketball star A.C. Green. Her son is almost as well known for his Christian witness and abstinence platform as for his all-time professional record of playing in more than 1,100 consecutive games.

ACCOMPLISHED MOTHERS

"Share your accomplishments with your child. The more your child senses that you value yourself, the greater the value your child will place upon you. And the greater he will value your expressions of love."

☞

—JAN DARGATZ

SOURCE: *52 Simple Ways to Tell Your Child "I Love You"* (Nashville, TN: Thomas Nelson Publishers/Oliver – Nelson, 1991)

CHOOSING VALUES AND STICKING BY THEM

I have core beliefs and values that are similar to my mother's and my grandmother's. My mother instilled in me a sense of community and the importance of giving back to the community and the value of self-sufficiency. I think these ideas are practical and mainstream ideas that don't change. They are my core values and are unchanging. Core values don't change. You don't develop your values and beliefs by checking with your friends, or by conducting polls and having focus groups. People will respect you if you are a person of character, integrity, and principle and if you hold firmly to those beliefs, regardless of popularity.

KAY COLES JAMES

Kay Coles James served as Virginia's Secretary of Health and Human Services, helping fashion one of the toughest welfare reform programs in the nation. She credits her mother (who raised six children alone after their father left them) with teaching her that responsibility for a family lies with the family itself and not with the government.

SOURCE: Washington and Lee University, www.wlu.edu

FULL HOUSE

"Fill your house with the Word,
and the house will fill up
with riches and wealth."

&

— MARILYN HICKEY

SOURCE: *God's Covenant for Your Family* (Tulsa: Harrison House, 1982)

FAMILY: A THEME THROUGHOUT THE BIBLE

- God's plan for marriage is presented in (Gen.2:24).
- In Exodus each commandment of the Decalogue touches upon behavior within the family circle.
- In Leviticus, the Law contains the death penalty for those who prostitute the home.
- In Numbers, the numbering of the people is done by family units (Num. 4:1, 2).
- Deuteronomy emphasizes parental instruction (Deut. 6:1-12)
- Joshua describes the godly patriarch who led his family to Yahweh God (Josh. 24:15); whereas Judges records the account of Samson's selfish, unbridled lust.
- Ruth records a beautiful story of romantic love and godly marriage. (Ruth 1:16,17)
- In the books of Samuel, Kings, and Chronicles, the history of Israel illustrates the influence of the home upon the kings. The wickedness of Ahab was extended and magnified by his wife Jezebel (1 Kings 21:5-16); whereas the greatness of Samuel and his unusual sensitivity to God certainly was partly due to the influence of the devout Hannah (1 Sam. 1:27, 28).
- In Ezra, Nehemiah, and Esther a godly seed was preserved through the family unit (Esth. 2:20; 4:14).
- Job reveals Satan's attack on the home through death, disease, poverty, and internal and internal strife (Job 1:13-21; 2:7-10).
- Psalms contains promises for the home (Ps. 127 and many others).
- Proverbs and Ecclesiastes abound in maxims about family and interpersonal relationships (Prov. 14:1; 22:6; Eccl. 4:9-12).
- The Song is an explicit account of a holy love between a man and a woman (Song 4:1-7).

- The prophetic books allude to the open violation of godly principles in families (Is. 3:12–26; Jer. 31:29-30; Lam. 4:10; Ezek. 16:44-45; Hos. 4:1-5; Joel 2:28, 29; Mic. 7:5-6; Mal. 2:14-16).
- In the New Testament, the synoptic Gospels present Jesus' teaching concerning the family (Matt. 19:3-9).
- John records his first miracle at a wedding in Cana (John 2:1-11).
- Acts makes mention of the home, together with the synagogue, as a center for worship (Acts 2:46; 12:12).
- The Epistles are full of teachings concerning the family. God commands husbands to love their wives as Christ loved the church by assuming leadership and responsibility. Wives were created to be helpers to their own respective husbands (Gen. 2:18), supplementing and not supplanting, complementing and commanding.
- Husbands and wives who enter parenthood are admonished to take seriously their responsibilities to teach God's Word to their children at every opportunity (Deut. 6:4-9; 20-25; Josh 4:6,7). Grandparents, aunts, uncles, and cousins were included in the extended family. The same loving commitment enjoined for husbands and wives is projected unto the generations (see Ruth 1:16, 17).

Adapted from THE WOMAN'S STUDY, *Dorothy Kelley Patterson, Ph.D., editor (Thomas Nelson, Nashville, Tennessee, 1995) Dr. Dorothy Patterson is married to former Southern Baptist Convention President Paige Patterson.*

THE STRENGTH OF HOME AND FAMILY

"… For the strength of a nation, especially of a republican nation, is in the intelligent and well-ordered homes of the people. And in proportion as the discipline of families is relaxed, will the happy organization of communities be affected, and national character become vagrant, turbulent, or ripe for revolution."

LYDIA H. SIGOURNEY,
LETTERS TO YOUNG LADIES, 1851

CHANGING NEIGHBORHOODS AND NATIONS

HATTIE HAMMOND

Hattie Hammond was ordained in 1927 at the age of 20, but by then her ministry was already in full swing. As a child, when her cousins came for a visit, they would play Sunday school and church, converting and baptizing all the dolls in the neighborhood.

In a tent meeting, a visiting evangelist saw her and went over and sat beside her. His name was John J. Ashcroft (grandfather of Attorney General John Ashcroft). She said, "I looked up at him ... and I said ... 'Brother, I am interested in the salvation of my soul...' Well, I hardly knew I had a soul and I did not know to say I was interested in the salvation of my soul. I didn't know what that meant but I knew I wanted God."

Soon Hattie was known as "the girl evangelist." By the 1930s, when she was still only in her 20s, she had become one of the most powerful speakers in the Pentecostal movement. Her message was simple, inspiring total abandonment and consecration to God. She served God faithfully until her death in the mid-1990s.

HONORING SPIRITUAL MOTHERS

I want to thank you Lord for the Spiritual Mothers in my life.
Each had a different talent and
was in my life for a different season.
They prayed for me. They listened to me. They helped me.
They cooked for me. They taught me.
They gave me counsel. They cried with me.
They cleaned me up when the shame nearly buried me.
They comforted me. They opened their homes to me.
They gave me a safe place to rest.
They gave me money when I was broke.
They spent hours on the phone with me.
They touched my life with truth.
They bound up my broken heart.
They freed me from the prison of guilt and confusion.
They turned on the light when darkness filled my mind.
They picked me up when I fell and encouraged me
when I was tired.
Without them I do not know where I would be.
They have been Jesus in the flesh to me.
They are the nature of Christ to me.
They reflect the voice of the Holy Spirit.
They are Wisdom dancing with Knowledge.
They are Understanding kissing Discernment.
They are the Presence of God in the sacrifice
of life's communion.
Thank you Lord for the blessing of Spiritual Mothers.

— LYNN WILFORD SCARBOROUGH

Lynn is an author, media coach and the director of Effective Television in Dallas,
Texas. She attributes her growth as a Christian to the "Spiritual Fathers and
Mothers" who have poured into her life and who work tirelessly around the globe
to bring souls into the fullness of Christ and knowledge of the Gospel.

DISCIPLINE, DIGNITY, DARING

At the tender age of eight, I was very ill. I overheard the doctor talk to my mother and father about my needing to be happier and to want to fight to get well. I opened my Bible and read Nehemiah 8:10: "The joy of the Lord is your strength." I knew then that God was showing me the way. He wanted me to get well and allow His joy to make me strong. Not my happy, giddy fleeting joy, but *His*. And His joy remains to this very day my strength!

The practice of regular routine demands a *discipline* of heart and mind. I will not allow a day to go by without His Word first. There will be a *dignity* about my life that is Christ-likeness. His Word gives me calmness of heart and security that makes me feel settled and dignified in Christ. Bold *daring* to be and to do is my aim for a Christ-centered, Bible-based, Spirit-filled life. I want to please Christ.

"Let us run with perseverance the race marked out for us" (Hebrews 12:1).

ℒ

MARILYN D. FRANCIS

Colonel Marilyn D. Francis is the women's organizations secretary for The Salvation Army's USA Eastern Territory. She oversees programs from Kentucky to Maine, as well in Puerto Rico and the Virgin Islands.

A WORLDWIDE MOVEMENT IS BORN

Back in 1957 a group of 70 or so women from Sydney, Australia, had an urge to go away together for a Bible study weekend. The event was such a life-changing experience for those women as they fellowshipped and studied God's Word together that they decided to do it again the next year. Many more ladies joined them. It was during that weekend that God spoke to the group about "lengthening their cords" and seeking ways of enabling women to come together in such a manner all over Australia. Christian Women's Conventions was born. From that small beginning the movement grew quickly across Australia. In 1972 a series of Bible studies was developed called Know Your Bible. Before very long more than 20,000 women across Australia were using this method of Bible study. And still the movement grew. Weekend and day conventions were a feature, as were luncheons, dinners, breakfasts and coffees. Seminars and workshops were developed. A ministry known as Safaris was established to evangelize and encourage women in remote areas of Australia. A Christian bookshop called "Book Nook" was opened in a suburb of Sydney. A Christian women's magazine was being produced by CWCI called "Christian Woman." A radio programme for women was developed beaming across airwaves around the globe.

Women were communicating the gospel message as never before. The movement now provided much more than the opportunity for women to come together at Conventions. The movement needed a name change. Christian Women Communicating International became the new name. Country by country CWCI grew. KYB studies have been translated and printed in Spanish, Kiswahili, Dutch, Russian, Danish, Chishona, Nepali, Indonesian,

Tok Pisin, Tamil, and Romanian. New studies are being written and translated each year. Around the world thousands of women's lives have been transformed through a relationship with Jesus Christ as they have come to know Him through attending a CWCI function and Know Your Bible study group.

&

MARGARET JACOBS

A national and international speaker with CWCI, Margaret Jacobs lives in Western Australia and is a Bible teacher, evangelist, and Bible college lecturer.

LEADERSHIP PROFILE

DELLA REESE

Reverend Della

She's well known as an actress, entertainer, and singer—easily recognized as the supervising angel in the Touched By An Angel series. But there's something less well known about Della Reese. She answers to "Reverend Della." In 1987 she was ordained as a minister and has founded Understanding Principles for Better Living Church (UP) in Los Angeles, a church whose aim is to lead and teach others to walk the walk of Jesus.

CHANGING NEIGHBORHOODS AND NATIONS

SUSANNAH WESLEY

The mother of 19 children, including John and Charles Wesley, Susannah Wesley (1669-1742) dedicated her large brood to God. The 13 child-rearing rules she laid down over 200 years ago have lost none of their currency today.

Susannah Wesley's Guide to Child-Rearing

- Eating between meals not allowed.
- As children they are to be in bed by 8 p.m.
- They are required to take medicine without complaining.
- Subdue self-will in a child, and those working together with God to save the child's soul.
- To teach a child to pray as soon as he can speak.
- Require all to be still during Family Worship.
- Give them nothing that they cry for, and only that when asked for politely.
- To prevent lying, punish no fault which is first confessed and repented of.
- Never allow a sinful act to go unpunished.
- Never punish a child twice for a single offense.
- Comment and reward good behavior.
- Any attempt to please, even poorly performed, should be commended.
- Preserve property rights, even in smallest matters.

SOURCE: www.victory-baptist.org

COLORING OUTSIDE THE LINES

THE FORMULA FOR SUCCESSFUL WOMEN IS:
God's purpose + God's gifts and talents =
focus, energy and joy without guilt.

When we know our God-given, unique purpose, and add to that our God-given talents and gifts, then we know where to invest our time, talent and treasure, and can live our lives in a way that is energized, focused and joyous, without feeling guilt.

Women have always helped fund the Kingdom of God. From the woman and her neighbors in the oil business (II Kings 4:1-7) to the Shunammite widow who provided a place of rest for a man of God (II Kings 4:8-37), to the women who traveled with Jesus (Luke 8:1-3), women have funded the Gospel out of their own means.

I was taught that "women are not supposed to be in leadership," and I took that as gospel. Then a mentor suggested that I make a list of every way my natural "gift" had been hindered in my life. When I finished and looked at the books I had been led to read, I found that they were about leadership! My friend's reaction was "Duh-uh!" God has created men and women unique to sing the distinctive song that He has placed within them. During the Atlanta Clergy Conference I was the only woman in the pastors' prayer room. It was an awesome and enlightening experience that forever changed my life.

Royal Treasure, an organization I founded in 1997, is a non-profit ministry to educate and equip women to become confident and competent in investing their treasure, time, and talent for the Kingdom. My dream is to see the greatest mobilization of Christian women stewards and the coming generation of generous

givers educated and motivated to move from "God-Prepared Hearts," to "God-Healed and Grateful Hearts," to "Overflowing Hearts," to "Praising and Worshiping Hearts."

⅊

Lu Dunbar

Lu Dunbar characterizes herself as "an investment counselor for the Kingdom," mentoring women in stewardship and the freedom to invest in advancing the kingdom of God.

OUR VOCATION

*"Many people mistake
our work for our vocation.
Our vocation is
the love of Jesus."*

— MOTHER TERESA OF CALCUTTA

SOURCE: Carroll E. Simcox, comp., *4400 Quotations for Christian Communicators*
(Baker Book House, Grand Rapids, Michigan, 1991)

IT'S NEVER TOO LATE FOR A WOMAN

At the age of 49, I tottered out of my dishpan and back to graduate school to work on what the Apostle Paul had to say to women. The Ph.D. took me until I was 61, but I began to find much fruitful material that could empower women in Christ's service.

"Where are our women scholars? Where are our women translators? Until we have this problem resolved, we shall have too many women given over to fashion and to folly." With these words of wisdom, Catherine Bushnell, a former missionary, became my mentor. She inspired me to pursue biblical truths about the ministry of women and God's response to abused women.

What happens when we look at Scripture through women's eyes? Are there ways in which the lives of both women and men can be enriched through such an effort? God called me to share insights that will send women empowered by the Word to bring the full implications of the gospel throughout the world.

&

CATHERINE KROEGER

Catherine Kroeger is adjunct association professor of classical and ministry studies at Gordon-Conwell Theological Seminary and co-editor of the IVP Women's Bible Commentary.

FINISHING STRONG

During a time when finishing high school was an accomplishment for women, my parents instilled in me the belief that there wasn't anything a woman couldn't do. I had seen the Great Depression. Through my mother and father, I had also seen high triumphs given to those who entrust their lives and the lives of their children—in our case five—to the Lord. With God as my navigator, I pursued my dreams.

Working my way through college, attaining three degrees, I found my career loves—speech, Christian education and journalism. As managing editor of *Christian Life* magazine from 1943 to 1948, I penned books and articles that were, and continue to be, read around the world. To this day, I am humbled that so mighty a God would allow me such advanced opportunities for women in that era.

In honor of my late husband, Dr. A. Berkeley Mickelsen, I must praise God for our wonderful 38 years of marriage. I could pull Berkeley's sleeve and say, "What does the original text say here?" With ease he would provide my answer. Berkeley read Greek as easily as he read English. Our marriage of skills and talents is exemplary of God's divine appointments in our lives. Berkeley was a fine scholar, but an unskilled writer. God used our combined skills to glorify Him to the maximum. At 82 years of age, I continue to write, teach, and speak—walking through whatever doors God opens. And God is good.

%

ALVERA MICKELSEN

Alvera Mickelsen's many works include THE FAMILY BIBLE ENCYCLOPEDIA *(later published as* Picture Bible Dictionary*);* UNDERSTANDING SCRIPTURE; WOMEN, AUTHORITY AND THE BIBLE; *and* STUDIES ON BIBLICAL EQUALITY.

STEPPING IN TO LEAD

In April, 1973 my husband suddenly went to be with the Lord. While his legacy lives on through his 250 books, it was I who the board asked to lead Christ for the Nations. By God's grace and His glory, CFNI has grown to become one of the largest full-gospel mission organizations in the world, reaching into 120 nations; helping to start 42 Bible schools worldwide; providing shipments of food, clothing, and medical aid to nations in crisis; supporting orphanages; ministering to prisoners; and providing scholarships for international students to attend Christ for the Nations Institute in Dallas. To date, our donors have helped us build nearly 10,850 native churches. One of them was the first church Dr. Yonggi Cho of Seoul, Korea pastored. His ministry has multiplied so that he now has the world's largest congregation— 750,000 members.

&

FREDA LINDSAY

Freda Lindsay is chairman emeritus of Christ For The Nations, Inc. At 87 years of age, she continues to work in her office daily.

TIME IS SHORT

"The most precious thing
a human being has to give is time.
There is so very little of it,
after all, in a life."

— EDITH SCHAEFFER

SOURCE: L'abri (Wheaton, IL: Tyndale House Publishers, 1969)

LEADERSHIP PROFILE

MAY FENG

A Place of Influence in China

Talk shows on radio and television. University lectures. Corporate and civic appearances. Family life conferences. Magazine columns. Tens of thousands of tapes in circulation. Discipleship of Christian women. It seems there's hardly a medium of communication that May Feng isn't using to reach the women and families of Taiwan.

Born in Taiwan, she immigrated to the United States at age 13. Converted to Christianity as a high-school sophomore, she soon became deeply involved in building a spiritual movement on her campus. After graduating from the University of Hawaii with a nursing degree in 1978, she returned to her homeland, where she and her husband, James Lee, have been serving with Campus Crusade ever since. James is now the ministry's national director for Taiwan. The couple has two sons, one in high school and one in college.

May lectures in four national universities on the topics of communication, relationships and family issues; hosts a weekly live call-in show on radio and appears monthly on a TV talk show; and, with her husband, coordinates family life conferences around Taiwan. Their family life tape series has sold over 160,000 copies. But May believes that discipling and training women is the foundation and core of all her ministries.

CHANGING NEIGHBORHOODS AND NATIONS

ROSA PARKS

*"Our mistreatment was just not right, and I was tired of it.
I kept thinking about my mother and my grandparents,
and how strong they were. I knew there was a possibility
of being mistreated, but an opportunity was being given
to me to do what I had asked of others."*

In 1955 this quiet but firm woman galvanized America's civil rights revolution when she refused to give up her seat on a bus to a white man. The subsequent 381-day Montgomery, Alabama, bus boycott, led by Martin Luther King, Jr., ended in 1956 after the U.S. Supreme Court ruled that bus segregation is unconstitutional. She has received the Presidential Medal of Freedom and the Congressional Gold Medal, among other honors.

Excerpt from ROSA PARKS, QUIET STRENGTH *(Zondervan Publishing House, 1994)*

THE PRIORITIES THAT ENHANCE YOUR MINISTRY

Jerry and I began our ministry with a meager budget, so we have never forgotten God's grace in our lives. Jerry loves to say that I have been his full partner in everything that has occurred during the past half century. Our little church of 35 people has grown to over 22,000 members, a worldwide television ministry, a multi-faceted educational institution, a global missionary effort, and a "salt ministry" which resulted in the creation of the Moral Majority and the "religious right."

I still treasure being a wife, mother, and grandmother more than anything. The Bible reminds us that where your heart is there is your treasure. My greatest treasure is in those precious lives God has entrusted to me.

To younger women involved in ministry and leadership, I encourage you: Guard your heart, your home, your husband, and your children. Protect your marriage and you will enhance your ministry. After 43 years of marriage, I can declare that the more you bless them now, the more you will hear them bless you in the future.

&

MACEL P. FALWELL

Macel Falwell is the wife of Jerry Falwell, chancellor of Liberty University in Lynchburg, Virginia.

ONE AUDACIOUS PRAYER, MILLIONS OF AMAZING ANSWERS

One day while I was still in my thirties, as I was deep in prayer, suddenly, seemingly from nowhere, I blurted out, "Lord, I want to teach the whole world to pray." Shocked at my audacity, I meekly begged God to forgive me. But now, over forty years later, I realize that that prayer came directly from God—because He has been fulfilling it ever since, proving what He does when women pray.

As that desire in my heart never lifted, I have stepped out in faith through every door He has opened. This has meant traveling overseas all alone, with limited physical strength, often close to bombs and hurricanes, even attacks by debilitating parasites. Through it all, I have seen that God raised up all the intercessors it would take to reach every continent personally with prayer training. God consistently answered their prayers and mine, proving to them the power of prayer much more amazingly than my teaching ever could.

I could never have imagined that God would open the doors to distribute millions of my books on prayer around the world and bring hundreds of thousands of women to our prayer seminars so they could become intercessors themselves in order to reach their worlds for Jesus.

&

EVELYN CHRISTENSON

The author of many books, Evelyn Christenson's book WHAT HAPPENS WHEN WOMEN PRAY? *has sold more than 1.5 million copies.*

LEADERSHIP PROFILE

ROMA DOWNEY

Assurance of God's Love

She tries to do more than portray an angel, "Monica" on *Touched By An Angel*. Roma Downey also tries to be an angel of sorts, a messenger of God's love. She says her favorite part of the show is when she is able to say, "I am an angel sent by God to tell you that God loves you." Roma believes everyone needs that assurance.

Off the set, she is busy as mom to her daughter, Reilly—and on the set as well. Reilly comes to the set for half of each taping day. Roma also spends time doing charity work with children, especially at Primary Children's Hospital in Salt Lake City. And, as she told an interviewer for the Lifetime network series *Intimate Portrait*, if it has to do with her Irish homeland, or children—and especially Irish children—then she'll be there.

SOURCE: Adapted from comments by Anna Kasper, Roma Downey Web pages.

WOMEN, ROLES AND CALLINGS

Ultimately, what you believe rules you. If you believe your life purpose is simply to fill limited roles, you'll fill them and stop there—never knowing more was available to you. You need to understand the difference between the roles you fill and the calling God has on your life.

A "role" is simply a set of expectations placed upon you by others based on your position. It is a temporary, natural-realm state that does not define who you truly are. For example, if you are an employee, it is expected that you carry out the duties of your position to the best of your ability. But when your job ends, you are no longer required to fill this role.

If you are a mother, it is expected that you feed, clothe, house and love your children and hopefully train them up "in the nurture and admonition of the Lord." But as your children grow, your mothering responsibilities change and gradually diminish until the kids are out on their own. Your true identity, on the other hand—who you are in Christ—never changes. We are eternal beings, and we cannot be defined by any position we hold in the natural, whether it be in the workplace, in the larger community or in the home.

Many years ago I made the mistake of defining myself by roles. When God opened the door for me and my husband, Steve, to begin our ministry in Christian publishing, I assumed the role of managing the company finances. Because of my position, I began to characterize myself and my ministry in a limited way. "I'm a businesswoman," I would say.

When presented with opportunities for ministry that didn't fit this mold, I was quick to point to someone I felt was more gifted to fill the slot. I believed I was already fulfilling my life purpose. After all, I was a wife, a mother and the chief financial officer in a ministry that was impacting many people for God.

In the early 1990's I became more hungry for God than I had ever been in my life. I sought Him continually. Soon I noticed that my love for Him was contagious and that new hunger was being birthed in those around me.

In that climate God began to speak to me about doing things for Him—such as mentoring other women and hosting prayer meetings in my home—that were foreign to me. They didn't fit with my narrow self-concept.

The more I pursued God, the larger and less comfortable His assignments became. When He first spoke to me about planning a women's conference, I immediately protested, "This must be a mistake. Don't You know who I am? I'm a businesswoman, not a platform minister."

But I found that my focus was wrong. As long as I looked at myself—my natural strengths and weaknesses—I wouldn't fulfill what God had for me to do. He was calling me to a new realm, a realm beyond natural ability, that would require total reliance on Him.

As I obeyed God and moved out beyond my comfort zone, the Holy Spirit led me step by step on a path that ultimately has ministered to thousands through conferences and "SpiritLed Woman" Magazine. He has given me assignments that in the natural I didn't understand, but when I have leaned on Him to fulfill them, He has allowed me to bear great fruit.

I feel even less prepared now to do the things He is asking of me, but I know that I can trust Him and that He can use the foolish and simple things for His glory (see I Cor. 1:27-28). You can trust Him, also. If you continue to say yes to Him in the face of every obstacle, He will work out His pleasure and will in your life (see Phil 2:13).

In the book of Acts, we are told that in the last days there will be a great outpouring of the Spirit of God that will transcend gender and age: "'And it shall be in the last days,' God says, 'That I will pour forth of My Spirit upon all mankind; and your sons and your daughters shall prophesy, and your young men shall see visions, and your old men shall dream dreams'" (Acts 2:17, NAS). I believe we are in that day. And you are destined to play a part!

℘

JOY STRANG

Joy Strang is the publisher of SpiritLed Woman magazine. The Strang Communications network she and her husband founded also includes CHARISMA, NEW MAN, MINISTRIES TODAY, *and other publications.*

WHAT IS LEADERSHIP?

*"Leadership is capitalizing
on a God-given window of opportunity
when it is presented. Not tepidly. Not timidly.
But boldly, by jumping into the fray with both
feet and a determination to change your world
with your ideas and your proposals."*

&

— MICHELLE EASTON

*Michelle Easton is head of the Clare Boothe Luce Policy Institute. This is
an excerpt from her speech to the Conservative Leadership Conference in
Alexandria, Virginia, November 17, 2000.*

TRANSFORMED THROUGH TRIALS

In 1975 I married Clint Murchison, Jr., founder and owner of the Dallas Cowboys football team. "Marry me, Annie. I'll smother you with kisses, and we'll live a life of bliss." I desperately wanted it to be true. I knew he had as much emotional pain as me, or more. I dreamed of us healing one another. The reality is, however, that hurt people hurt people.

We lived in a 44,000-square-foot house in the middle of twenty-six beautifully landscaped acres. We had five Mercedes, an island in the Bahamas, a penthouse on Park Avenue in New York. None of these luxuries quenched my neediness. To make matters worse, my closest friends responded to my despondence with, "What do you have to be depressed about?" Most of us believe that money and possessions equal happiness. I quickly learned that they do not. Having these things only escalated my hopelessness.

Clint and I loved each other deeply. We were alike yet separated by a great chasm, just beyond the other's reach. Our needs were too great. To my disappointment, neither of us knew how to heal ourselves, much less the other.

I ran into a distant friend, Janis Coffee, at a political fundraiser. She invited me to hear her testimony at Christian Women's Club. February 12, 1976, I tearfully surrendered my life to Jesus Christ. Janis began teaching a small Bible study in my home.

Immediately I fell in love with the Word of God. Two years after my conversion I began to give my testimony and teach the Bible. I published two books, *Milk for Babes* in 1978 and *Praise and Worship* in 1980. Yet I still hurt.

One morning on my knees, I looked toward heaven and cried out, "Lord, you said truth sets us free. Teach me, Lord. Set me free." Little did I realize it would take me so long to learn or that the path of growth would be so difficult.

In 1981 my mother died. Doctors diagnosed Clint with cerebellar atrophy. His prognosis was a slow and tragic death. I felt like I was drowning all the time. We searched God's Word to insure we were obeying Him. We asked people we hurt to forgive us. We forgave those who hurt us. We confessed our sins to one another. We more than tithed our money. Two Bible studies a week met in our home. Our doors opened wide to everyone. The elders of our church anointed Clint with oil and prayed for his healing. Multitudes prayed for us.

By 1984 Clint was in a wheel chair. To further complicate our lives, he had serious financial problems. After he sold the Cowboys in 1985, his creditors began to worry because of his condition. They put him in bankruptcy. His was the largest personal bankruptcy in the history of the nation at that time. Our problems were splashed across the front pages of the nation's newspapers and periodicals. Unbearable pressures crowded on every side. There was nowhere to run.

Somewhere along the way a gentle voice interrupted my insanity. "Come unto me," my Savior said. In the midst of my daily diatribes, God's unconditional love inched into every available crack and crevice of my hardened heart. I have never been the same.

Clint died in 1987. God transformed him through our trials too. We shared tears and more love and tenderness in those last years of his life than either of us had ever known. Though bittersweet, those were the most precious of times between us.

ℒ

ANNE MURCHISON

Anne Murchison is a writer, lecturer and Bible teacher. She has two adult children and three grandchildren. She lives in East Texas.

LEADERSHIP PROFILE

JANE HUCKABY

Helping Open Doors

After reading Brother Andrew's book, *God's Smuggler*, Jane was inspired by the challenge to "awaken and strengthen what remains and is at the point of death" (Rev. 3:2). She committed herself to serve through Open Doors and today is director of operations at Open Doors USA, overseeing the day-to-day duties (computers, phones, donor relations, etc.) of this international ministry to the suffering church. She also serves as the Director of Women of the Way, a new program at Open Doors designed to mobilize women across the US to strengthen persecuted Christians. She has been serving in Christian nonprofit ministries since 1989, when, as vice president at the Christian Research Institute she began a six-year period of overseeing the radio outreach of *The Bible Answerman*.

With Open Doors, Jane has seen firsthand the suffering of Christians from Peru and Colombia to Iran and Pakistan. She shares the stories of her persecuted brothers and sisters with groups throughout North America. As a single woman, she cherishes the flexibility to go wherever, whenever God calls.

MINISTERING ON DEATH ROW

"Nothing can prepare you perfectly for ministry to Death Row inmates," says Order of the Founder member Major Kathryn Cox, who [has ministered] on the Row since 1986. She says God prepared her for such a ministry by developing in her a strong spirit of compassion and understanding. Her undergraduate degrees in psychology and journalism and master's degree in criminal justice help her as she also coordinates Bible correspondence courses for 30,000 inmates through the Army's Texas division and in her work with the families of condemned prisoners . . . What she has learned not only makes hers an informed voice on such issues as the death penalty and the legal rights of prisoners, but guides her as she tends to her eternal standing before God. What she has witnessed attests mightily to a salvation that can penetrate any locked door.

୧

FROM THE SALVATION ARMY WAR CRY,
AUGUST 5, 2000

THE VISION WASN'T MINE ALONE

In the spring of 1994 there was a scheduled regional meeting of the Episcopal Daughters of the King in Yorktown, Virginia. Women from three states were to gather to pray, to worship, and to learn of the attributes of a servant of our Lord. The scheduled guest speaker was noted for his sound theological presentation mixed with charismatic enthusiasms. His wife and partner in ministry for the day was celebrated for her musical talents which entered the ears and pierced the heart.

The weather was to be beautiful, the women enthusiastic, the speaker well known, the publicity campaign efficient, the anticipation was high. It was to be a good meeting.

The day arrived with an attendance meager to the point of discouragement, yet those in attendance were a holy group. The music began. Our Lord's hand was upon the musician's skilled ability on the piano and combined with her voice allowed us to enter into that spiritual Holy of Holies where earth and heaven meet. As "Commune with Me" began to fill the air around me, a strange inward occurrence followed.

Tears began to course down my cheeks. My heart became so hot that I thought my hand would be burned if it touched my chest. My heart became "enlarged." It felt as if it consumed my entire chest and became so heavy that I had to kneel. As I sank under the weight, my mind was racing. *What is happening to me? Am I having a heart attack?* Yet, I knew instantaneously that I was not suffering from a normal happenstance. My prayer, as I descended to my knees was: "O, Lord, do not let me be put to shame and do not allow others to sin in their condemnation of this action." Not all in attendance that day approved of the "charismatic" gifts.

I lingered in prayer as the music continued. The moment of heat and weight passed. I looked up to see the empty church filled with women in prayer! Women were looking in the windows, women were standing along the back and in the aisles. I could even see behind to the door where women waited to enter. Christians, the true Bride of Christ, of all shapes and sizes, color and expression of faith had come to minister to God in the Holy of Holies.

The vision lasted a lifetime, and yet only seconds. I stood, shaken but calm, to continue with the meeting, knowing that my life would never be the same, for God had shown me His heart's desire.

In the fall of 1997, the first Tapestry Day of Prayer was held at the National Cathedral in Washington, D.C. Over 800 women from all denominations were gathered for prayer—all sitting side by side participating in a service centered on the historic hours during which our Lord Jesus gave His life on the cross. What God had shown in a vision in 1994 became a living reality three years later.

The speakers and workshop leaders were from all denominations. The surprise, however, was to be told by Vonette Bright, Dee Jepsen, Bobbye Byerly, Evelyn Christensen, and others that this was an answer to their 15-year-long prayer. God had prepared the way long before I was shown the vision!

&

BONNIE SHANNONHOUSE

Founded by Bonnie Shannonhouse, Tapestry has gone on to have Days of Prayer in churches from coast to coast and on five continents. Bonnie is the author of THE LOST COIN *series, books detailing the disciplined prayers of Jesus' day and of the early church.*

VIRTUE BY NECESSITY

"It is not in the still calm of life,
or in the repose of a pacific station,
that great challenges are formed ...
Great necessities call out great virtues."

℮

— ABIGAIL ADAMS, LETTER TO HER HUSBAND
JOHN ADAMS, JANUARY 19, 1780

SOURCE: *Familiar Quotations* by John Bartlett.

WOMEN, SETTING THE STANDARD FOR MISSIONS

Overall, probably two-thirds of the total force for missions has been, and currently is, female. Many mission executives agree that the more difficult and dangerous the work, the more likely women are to volunteer to do it!

Some fear that with the unique obstacles of reaching the Muslim world, Western women can play no part. Yet in a nomadic Muslim group in Sub-saharan Africa, a single woman is effectively training imams (Muslim teachers) in the Gospel. They perceive her to be non-threatening, "just a woman." Building upon a foundation of interpersonal relationship and Bible knowledge, she does not give them answers herself. She simply shows the imams how to find them in the Word. The Lord has confirmed her teaching, giving dreams and visions to these leaders. As they have been converted, they are now training many others.

Women, stirred by the task that lies ahead, can mobilize, devoting their skills, their accessibility, their knowledge, their tenderness, their intuitiveness, their own distinctive fervor to the work. The pioneer spirit, full of dedications and faithfulness, which women throughout history have shown, will set the standard. The task is too vast to be completed without all God's people!

2

MARGUERITE KRAFT AND MEG CROSSMAN

Marguerite Kraft served as a missionary to the Kamwe people of Nigeria. She is now professor of anthropology and linguistics at the School of Intercultural Studies at Biola University. Best known as a mission mobilizer and coordinator of the Perspectives course in Arizona, Meg Crossman was the executive director of I.C.A.R.E. prison ministries for 10 years.

Excerpted from Worldwide Perspectives, edited by Meg Crossman, 1996. Used by permission of William Carey Library.

KATHERINE KERSTEN

Spokeswoman for a Different Way

She's a regular columnist in the Minneapolis *Star Tribune* and a commentator for National Public Radio's *All Things Considered*. She's been sought out for her views by NPR's *Talk of the Nation* and Canadian Broadcasting Company's *As It Happens*. Her work has been discussed in publications from Honolulu, Hawaii, to Cairo, Egypt. Katherine Kersten's writings include "What Do Women Want? A Conservative Feminist Manifesto" and "The Politicization of Minnesota's Public School Curriculum."

An attorney as well as a writer, she has served as chairman of the Center of the American Experiment and vice president of the Institute on Religion and Democracy. Married to attorney Mark Johnson, she is a mother at home with four children, one of whom she home schools.

WOMEN IN MINISTRY? YES!

The traditional role of women in churches is being challenged to its very foundation as we move ahead in this new millennium. Today as never before, many women are finally coming into their rightful place in the body of Christ and restoring to the body a wonderful sense of great unity and completeness. This is the sort of unity that makes the church powerful and it is seen in the early church when men and women laboured together to fulfil the Great Commission.

I believe that the misunderstanding of the role of women in the church has come about because many have tried to apply the scriptural role of women in the home to their role in the church. Firstly, if we examine the role of the women in the home we will find that it is very clearly designated as one of "submission." Biblical submission is a way that God provides protection, not abuse, for the woman. Clearly God has defined that the man should be the head, or the authority, in the home as he provides, guards, protects, nurtures, and loves his wife and family. As this man loves his wife the way Christ loves the church, which literally means he would be willing to lay down his life for her, she will have no problem with respecting his headship in her home. His love for her will protect her from his making decisions that will in any way lord it over her. He gives his children a heritage of which they can be proud as he stands in that place of headship, for it has been said that no greater gift can a man give his children than to love their mother.

Spiritually mature women have no problem with this divine order God implemented in the structure of the family unit. Everything in our lives will function well if we keep our priorities as firstly God, then our husband, children, home, work, and finally our ministry.

When Jesus ascended on high He gave gifts unto men (Eph. 4:8). The term "men" is more aptly translated "mankind," which consists of both genders, male and female. These gifts that Christ left to the church were for the equipping of the saints and the building of the body of Christ until we all come into that place of unity in the faith of one Lord, one Spirit and one God. Jesus never intended them to be the sole domain of the male. The body of Christ is made up of men and women, and it is folly for anyone to think that men must always be the custodians of these five-fold ascension gifts, other ministry gifts or any of the gifts of the Holy Spirit!

All through the Bible we see women mightily used by God. He chose Deborah to be judge of Israel and used her to change a whole nation (Judges 4:14). God chose Esther to courageously stand in the face of certain death, should she fail, to be the vessel through which He saved the nation of Israel from destruction. Paul listed 12 women as part of his ministry teams fulfilling various functions. Few seemed to be of helps ministry, but rather front-line ministries with women in many positions of authority (Rom. 16).

God is bringing many women to the fore, right alongside His faithful and secure men who are not threatened by a woman with the same God-given call on her life as he has on his! The calls are not unique to men and God never wanted them to be. If indeed God only wanted men in positions of ministry He would actually have violated His own Word, which says He changes not. God looks on the heart; the spirit of the person whom He appoints, He anoints and equips for the task.

Throughout my tennis career I always trained and practiced with men. Never once did I feel inferior, unworthy, or out of place with them. I was equal to them—not in a physical sense, but in a sense of fulfilling my destiny right alongside them fulfilling theirs. And they never once thought of me as inferior to them for they simply respected the gift and talent in me. The church could learn from the principles seen here—that it is always the call upon your life and the anointing that goes with the call to fulfill the "gift in you" that makes room for you, regardless of whether you are male or female.

$\mathcal{L}$

MARGARET COURT

Margaret Court is a pastor, teacher, and ministry leader in her native Australia. As an international tennis champion, she won more than 60 Grand Slam titles.

CHANGING NEIGHBORHOODS AND NATIONS

MARCELLA OF ROME

Marcella of Rome (A.D. 325–410) turned her palatial home into a Christian retreat, invited famous leaders of the church to teach and held Bible studies. She established the first convent in the West.

Adapted from Lorry Lutz, WOMEN AS RISK TAKERS FOR GOD *(Baker Books, Grand Rapids, Michigan, 1997)*

MY PROVERBS 31 WOMEN

I never wanted to read the Bible again!

Feeling very out of place, I remember walking into the back door of a church for the first time. One woman who was in leadership in the church came to me with her Bible open. She told me that God laid me on her heart, "If Michele would become like the Proverbs 31 woman, how God would bless her life!" Well, if God had a blessing for me, I wanted to know what page it was on! Later that day, alone in my bedroom, I opened the Bible for myself. As I read through the description of this wonderful woman in the book of Proverbs, a knot began to form in my stomach. I realized that it would be impossible for me to be anything like her. I saw myself as damaged, flawed beyond repair.

"The letter of the law kills," the Scriptures say. Though her intentions were good, the church lady almost killed any spark of life that was in me. By contrast, the first time I met a Proverbs 31 woman I couldn't stop watching her. I wondered how anyone could become so loving and lovely. To my eyes she was, "like apples of gold in settings of silver," a word *fitly* spoken. Just as Jesus was the good Word about God in a package people could understand, so Christian women can make His ways knowable, acceptable, and winsome by their lives.

The first Proverbs 31 woman in my life is the woman I know now as mother-in-law. I call her my mother-in-love. In order to appreciate her you must understand that she and her husband were precious Christians. They were wearing their knees out praying for their wayward son to meet one of those nice girls from church who would turn his heart back to Christ. But who did he bring home? The spicy little number in a hip-hugger mini-skirt.

To her credit, when my boyfriend's mother opened the door of her home, she opened the door of her heart to me. I was welcomed into her home and into her life. This, I learned later, was her irresistible strategy to love me into the kingdom. In such an environment of love, it was only a short time before I accepted the Savior.

As an abused and abandoned child, I was left alone with a daddy I loved, who was perverse, alcoholic, and full of anger. I, of all people, needed a mentor. My daddy's raging and gross lack of parenting abilities led me to the point of suicide. But just in time, someone introduced me to a loving heavenly Father through Christ.

When my new husband and I moved to a strange town, the mentor I had in my mother-in-law was miles away. God sent Anna, my second Proverbs 31 mentor. Anna was an ordinary woman who laid a foundation for all that I am, all that I do.

Feeling lonely, rejected and awkward in this new town, Anna introduced herself to me. She commented that she was a widow, alone a lot, and would like to sit with me in church. Something in her expression reminded me of my mother-in-love. I was delighted that someone accepted me enough to want to sit with me.

Anna invited me to visit around her kitchen table regularly. Every time I left her home I was encouraged, instructed and challenged. Her Bible was our textbook. Anna shared about her life of struggles, of faith and faithfulness. She overflowed with love for Jesus—for everyone, it seemed. Her help was practical, and deliberate. She seemed to know what the next step or topic should be for me. Anna often did not answer my questions, she taught me how to get my questions answered. And she always gave me the bigger picture. Anna taught me that I was under the direct and specialized training of God to be at work in His vineyard, that as He poured Himself into her, she would pour herself into me, with the understanding that I was to do the same for others.

Many years later in my ministry to women, I realized that Anna had mentored me in Titus 2 fashion, and that skills I learned from a master builder equipped me for a life of joy and service. Because of her life investment in me, I can look women in their hurting eyes and promise them that the Savior is able to take what's left of life's worst abuses and fashion joy, beauty, strength and service ... for His glory.

ℒ

MICHELE RICKETT

Michele Rickett is director of Sisters in Service, Partners International. She has gathered the lessons Anna taught her into a nine-month Bible-study course aimed at graduating trained mentors.

FROM MAN'S KINGDOMS
TO GOD'S ARMY

"God is removing the 'flesh programs'
in our lives and churches, and tearing
down man's kingdoms in order for the
new generation to be what God wants it
to be. He is cleansing the Church; changing her
motivation, attitudes, priorities and
character; and training her to be His army."

&

—FUCHSIA PICKETT,
THE NEXT MOVE OF GOD

TRUST GOD
WHEN ALL ELSE HAS GONE

Lietnom, a town in Southern Sudan, is not too far from the front line. For nearly 20 years war has raged between the fundamentalist Muslim north and the Christian/animist south. Here there are no modern conveniences. In a country the size of the U.S. east of the Mississippi, there are only around 12 miles of paved road. There is no currency to own. People barter in chickens, ears of corn or maybe a small piece of rag. Mosquitoes bite like they do nowhere else I have visited. Malaria is rampant. Ninety-five percent of the population are women and children. The men are either dead or away on the frontline. Clothes are scarce and health and educational facilities are only there because of World Relief. Yet the church is exploding with life. The women and children are turning to Christ. This is probably the fastest church growth in the world. Yet every day women will wake up to desperate conditions with, humanly speaking, no hope and yet an assurance of God's love for them.

Does my faith match up?

I think of Debbie. As a young American wife, pregnant with her first baby, she and her husband went to Ethiopia to do an internship with a hospital there. One day while she was working in the hospital, some Eritrean rebels broke in and captured Debbie along with another nurse, Anna. Within 100 yards of the hospital, Anna was shot dead. For four weeks Debbie was held captive. Moved around with guns to her head, yet at the same time feeling her baby move within her womb, she trusted God. Today, Debbie and Carl live in Kenya, their home for over 20 years. Debbie has given her life to work with those who are dying from AIDS. She could be here in the U.S., maybe earning "mega bucks," but instead is serving her Lord far from home.

I could tell you of countless women who have a level of faith that makes mine seem so paltry. Perhaps meeting Rhoda in Malawi sums it up for me. I went to visit her in her pitiful hovel of a home. It was tiny and made of mud. Due to the weather and her being unable to spend money on her home, one of the walls had collapsed. The day I saw her, her bucket had been stolen, so there was no means of collecting water. Her home had no furniture. I sat on her mud floor. Rhoda was blind. In her arms she cradled a very sickly granddaughter dying from AIDS. Her own daughter had recently died from this disease. Her only source of income was to beg on street corners. As I spoke with her, I asked, "What would you like me to tell the women in the west about your situation?" Her response will be one I will never forget until my dying day. She said, "Tell them what you have seen and tell them I have Jesus and He is all I need!"

I see women trusting God when all else has gone. I see women starting small businesses through the loan of $50—a program that is transforming the lives of countless people in those countries where we have been able to develop community "banks." I see the hunger for those dying from AIDS to "gossip Jesus" to their neighbours and friends. When they are facing heaven imminently, the tongues just tell of the Jesus they love and serve.

The list is endless. How does my love for Jesus stand up against such circumstances? Perhaps it is best for me to stay silent!

&

RUTH CALVER

Ruth Calver has ministered to war-torn villages, London theater troupes, AIDS victims, drug addicts, and abandoned youth. Her husband, Clive, is president of World Relief.

PRAY GLOBALLY...

FOR YOUR SISTERS WHO LIVE IN FEAR OF DOWRY DEATHS

Where arranged marriages and dowry practices exist, women who are unable to meet the demands for gifts or money sometimes sacrifice their own lives through suicide, or die at the hands of a husband or his family. Recently, a woman in Vanasthalipuram, India, was murdered, set ablaze with kerosene, after she refused to seek more dowry from her father.

The number of dowry deaths reported nationwide in India rose from 5,513 to 6,917 in a recent two-year period. It is alleged that many more deaths are fabricated to be accidents. Despite the appalling number of women killed each year, demands for increased dowry payments escalate. The family of the bride must meet the demand or risk the death of their daughter, often perpetrated by the mother-in-law or sister-in-law of the victim of the "accident."

- Pray for the establishment of an inheritance system as a substitute.
- Pray for local leaders and ministers to denounce the custom.
- Pray for new incentives to arise that will make keeping women alive more profitable than killing us!

WOMEN OF PRAYER

In his epistle, Paul sets a blueprint for women of God today. He first points out to the fledgling church at Ephesus, the blessings they possess through the Lord Jesus and the place they have in God. These they obtained only because of the atonement and righteousness of Christ. Here, Paul is casting a mind-boggling vision of who we are in Christ. Then he proceeds to exhort us not only to accept, but understand the responsibility of walking in the light of our inheritance in Christ Jesus. In short, it is a plea to fill the world with the presence of the Master.

Paul's selfless prayer is a call to extend faithfully the hope Christ offers to those who are hopeless in nations all around us. This is also a commission that tears down all limits concerning us – so you and I have no excuse whatsoever to shirk our responsibility through prayer.

Once we realize who we are in Christ, our lives are to reflect that transformed identity as we prayerfully help others share the truth we hold dear. Then we can seriously own the responsibility of bringing into reality God's purpose for His world.

With clarity of vision, we must execute that divine will, through the power of God working within us to transform our world as we follow the Apostle Paul's example in fervent prayer. May we pray with passion and tenacity even as Jacob did when he wrestled with God. Let us catch the vision of being called and chosen for transformation through prayer.

&

NITA EDWARDS

Nita Edwards is a radio broadcaster, seminar teacher and writer. She serves as International Director of ASIA ALIVE GLOBAL, which operates a Prayer Center in Virginia and ministers to unreached people groups in 17 Asian nations.

THE FAITH OF A CHILD

James has often described our younger daughter, Robin, as "high energy," "strong spirited," and "determined to the end." Even now, as a wife and mother of three, we are amazed at Robin's creative drive to organize her family and household to live in the fullness of God's plan.

When Robin was eleven years old, she taught us all an incredible lesson of faith. An unsightly tumor began to grow on the left side of her bottom lip. James and I were immediately concerned and had our family doctor examine it. He felt it was not dangerous, but encouraged us to have a specialist remove it. I was disappointed when the specialist told us that he would not be able to schedule the procedure for weeks. After we left the doctor's office, Robin decided that the delay was a sign that God was going to heal her miraculously.

I was amazed and surprised by Robin's faith. Even though our family had been learning to trust God for miracles and healing in our personal lives and ministry, I was taken aback by my young daughter's resolve.

Extended family and close friends were encouraged by Robin's faith and joined us in praying for healing. I, too, had studied God's Word and believed that He still healed people supernaturally. I knew I could trust Him for healing in my own body and for others. Yet, when my own children are suffering, I tend to want Him to fix everything, and fast!

I prayed day and night for Robin's healing, but as the weeks went by, my faith began to falter. Every time I looked at that grotesque tumor on my beautiful daughter's lip, my heart ached. Robin, however, went through her days as if the tumor didn't exist.

Her faith was incredible! I didn't want to discourage her, so when I was having a "low moment," I would go off to my closet, shut the door, and cry out to God in desperation.

To make matters worse, Robin's school had a special program scheduled, and she had a significant part to perform. She was confident that the tumor would be gone by then. The week before the school program, I began putting intense pressure on God to "Do something!" because I couldn't stand it any longer. That night I went to bed very discouraged. As my restlessness gave way to sleep, I found myself in the midst of a dream that was so real that I perceived it to be a word from God. In the dream, I saw Robin coming into our bedroom holding the tumor in her hand.

The next morning, I eagerly rushed into Robin's room, hoping to see that the tumor was gone. It wasn't. I was heartbroken, but I still shared my dream with Robin. Her excitement about my dream moved her to an even higher level of faith. Later that day, as I walked past her bedroom door, I heard Robin talking aloud. I called through the door, "Honey, who are you talking to?" Robin answered, "I'm practicing my testimony so I'll know just what to say when God heals me." I smiled bravely and made a quick exit so that she would not see me cry.

A few days later, as James was preparing to leave town for a meeting, he said, "Betty, I feel that God wants us to pray a very specific prayer about the tumor. I think Robin and I need to trust God to heal her by this Friday." This was only a few days away. I admired Robin and James's big step of faith, and I begged God to come through for my daughter.

On Friday morning, Robin was awakened by her hand slapping her face, right on her bottom lip, where the tumor was. When she opened her eyes, she saw what she perceived to be an angel, kneeling by her bedside. As Robin got up, she saw something lying on the sheets. It was the tumor. She quickly looked into the mirror and saw only a tiny red spot on her lip where the tumor had been. She ran into my room shouting, "Mom, it's gone! It's gone!" as she showed me the tumor in her hand.

"Oh, Jesus, thank you!" I rejoiced. Robin was healed just in time for the school program, and she testified before the whole school about her special miracle from God.

When you're faced with a difficult or seemingly impossible situation, remind yourself of the faith of a child. Children trust their parents to make the best choices on their behalf. In the same way, God's intervention, whether through supernatural means, is always in our best interest. Make a decision today to fill your heart with faith that He will come through—one way or another, one day or another.

☙

BETTY ROBISON

Betty Robison and her husband, James, head the international evangelistic ministry Life Outreach International. This essay is an excerpt from her devotional book, WOMEN AT THE WELL *(Life Publications, 2001).*

DARE TO BELIEVE IN HIS PURPOSE FOR YOU

It is my privilege to serve in a ministry of women, for women, for the past 30 years. I have watched in my own life and the lives of many other women how God takes ordinary women, real people with real problems, and does a transforming work in their lives as well as those around them.

Throughout history, women who make themselves available to His power and grace have been used by God to shape and change neighborhoods, cities, and nations, offering hope, faith, love, courage, and wisdom. Age, background, race—they don't matter. Each woman has a plan, purpose and destiny, as God has demonstrated in His Word. Think of Mary, who through obedience brought forth the Son of God. Esther, who through courage saved her people. Deborah, who through wisdom led an army and portrayed the strength of the male and female role. Rahab, who through faith and an act of kindness saved her household. Think of the woman at the well, who through repentance became the first woman evangelist and won her city.

God is no respecter of persons. Put your name on this list of heroes and dare to believe Him to complete your purpose and destiny.

℘

CAROL TORRANCE

Carol Torrance is a member of the U.S. board of Aglow International.

WHAT A WOMAN
WANTS DONE IS DONE!

Growing up in the "Builder Generation," I thought being born of the female gender provided for the greatest opportunities and satisfactions of life. My mother taught me that there are no limits to what a woman can accomplish. What a woman wants done is done! A woman's inspiration and influence in the lives of men can challenge them to great heights or plunge them to despair. In addition, infinite possibilities exist for a woman to influence the lives of children, especially her own.

From the beginning of our marriage, my husband made me a full partner. On our honeymoon, he said, "I married you as Vonette Zachary; you are just adding Bright to your name. I want you to remain who you are." When God gave the vision for Campus Crusade for Christ, it was Bill's idea to name me co-founder. I left a teaching position with the Los Angeles city schools to join Bill in ministry.

In the late 1950s and early '60s I became concerned about how our culture was changing. Ruth Graham was one of a number of Christian women I asked what we, as Christian women, might do to make a difference. Seeing the need to mobilize Christian women to pray led to the Great Commission Prayer Crusade, which I chaired. All across the United States and Canada the crusade staff and I began to mobilize women to pray.

Billy Graham called for a congress on evangelism in Lausanne, Switzerland, in the early '70s. The Lord began to open doors for me, "the girl Bill married," to have influence worldwide. It began when I became one of three women to serve on a committee of 50 people from the Lausanne congress. Then, in 1984, the International Prayer Assembly in Seoul, Korea, brought 3,000 people from 71 countries to join 100,000 Koreans to pray for our changing world. I remained with this committee for 14 years, chairing the Intercession Working Group the last ten of those years.

God's provision allowed me to put my family first while answering His call, and a wonderful Christian woman came to live with us. Hard and long hours were exciting challenges for me, as long as I could keep Bill and the children as the number-one priority. Much of the time, I worked after the children were in bed. My schedule was adjusted to meet their needs and their schedules.

This year we are celebrating the 50th year of the founding of Campus Crusade for Christ. We have a new president, though we will continue to be involved as the Lord directs. We are not retiring, but refining. My husband's health is a challenge as he has pulmonary fibrosis. We are learning to know and trust the Lord in a new way, and our relationship is more meaningful than ever. While we don't know what the future holds, we know it will be rich, wonderful, and blessed by the hand of God. We are claiming Isaiah 58:11, knowing that His way is perfect.

Early in our marriage, we signed a contract to be slaves of Jesus. That contract will continue until our last breath on earth and first breath in heaven. To God be praise.

"The Lord will guide you continually,
And satisfy your soul in drought,
And strengthen your bones;
You shall be like a watered garden,
And like a spring of water, whose
Waters do not fail." (Is. 58:11 NKJV)

℘

VONETTE BRIGHT

As chairman of the National Day of Prayer Task Force, Vonette Bright in 1988 helped introduce legislation unanimously approved by both houses of Congress to make the first Thursday of every May the permanent date for the National Day of Prayer.

WOMEN ARE HOPE-GIVERS

*"Hope is the essential ingredient
to make it through life.
It is the anchor of the soul."*

BARBARA JOHNSON

SOURCE: *Stick a Geranium in Your Hat and Be Happy*
(Dallas: Word Books, 1990)

"God does not give women spiritual
blessings to keep to themselves.
He gives them to edify others, to enrich
His Kingdom, and to accomplish
His purposes through us ...
There is no reason why you cannot
become all God created you to be.
You can be as great as any biblical hero
or heroine, but there are obstacles you
will have to overcome just as they did.
If you can become convinced
in your heart that God loves you,
nothing can stop you from achieving
His purposes for your life."

—NANCY CORBETT COLE,
THE UNIQUE WOMAN

NANCY CORBETT COLE CHARITIES

A portion of the proceeds from this book will be given to Nancy Corbett Cole Charities, serving the abused, addicted and abandoned. Internationally, "Nancy Corbett Cole Homes of Refuge" provide housing, vocational training and education for abused women and children. In the United States, help is ongoing on an individual and corporate basis.

Nancy Corbett Cole, "The Loveliest Lady in the Land," supported her husband, Edwin Louis Cole, in pursuing his life's mission for 54 years. One of her most endearing mini-teachings was, "You have more than you think you do. You can do more than you think you can. You alone are responsible to use the talents, gifts and abilities God has given you." Behind the scenes, she was a spiritual anchor and provider for many.

By purchasing this book, you have helped society's underserved and less privileged members. If this book helped you, please consider sending a generous donation as well. Your one-time or continual support will help the helpless, heal the hurting, and relieve the needy. Your gift is fully tax-deductible in the U.S. Send your compassionate contribution to:

Nancy Corbett Cole Charities
P. O. Box 92501
Southlake, TX 76092 USA

Thank you for your cheerful and unselfish care for others.

INDEX

Watch for More Watercolor Books™ by Authors Like:

EDWIN LOUIS COLE

NANCY CORBETT COLE

G. F. WATKINS

DONALD OSTROM

and many more!

WWW.WATERCOLORBOOKS.COM

FOR INTERNATIONAL ORDERS
OR PUBLISHING, CONTACT
ACCESS SALES INTERNATIONAL
WWW.ACCESS-SALES.COM
OR
DIANAE@ACCESS-SALES.COM

WOMEN HELPING WOMEN

To become a hope-giver in the 21st Century, and receive help to change nations and neighborhoods, the editors have created a FREE "Woman's Guide" to help you find God's will for your life and mobilize you right where you are. Write or call today, and you'll also receive a FREE copy of the Declaration from the "Global Celebration for Women" held at the Houston Astrodome in 2001.

Log on to make your request at www.watercolorbooks.com.

Or, send your name and address to
Watercolor Books
P. O. Box 93234
Southlake, TX 76092.

Or, call toll-free 1-844-4888.

For further information on your favorite writers from
A Celebration of Women, and many more, go to
www.networkofchristianwomen.org (or, www.nocw.org).